Teachers' Guide

EDUCATIONAL   PUBLISHING

Story-writing
SCAFFOLDS

ria Roberts

HOPSCOTCH

1904 307396 1689 40

Published by
Hopscotch Educational Publishing Ltd
Unit 2
The Old Brushworks
56 Pickwick Road
Corsham
Wiltshire
SN13 9BX
Tel: 10249 701701

© 2003 Hopscotch Educational Publishing

Written by Christine Butterworth and Maria Roberts
Series design by Blade Communications
Cover illustration by Kirsty Wilson
Illustrated by Jane Bottomley
Printed and bound by Athenaeum Press, Gateshead

ISBN 1-904307-39-6

Christine Butterworth and Maria Roberts hereby
assert their moral right to be identified as the
authors of this work in accordance with the
Copyright, Designs and Patents Act, 1988.

Story-writing SCAFFOLDS

CONTENTS

Story-writing Scaffolds for Year 5

INTRODUCTION

Story-writing Scaffolds for Year 5 is intended for use in schools to help teach children how to write effective short stories in a variety of different genres. It improves children's ability to organise their writing so that it has purpose by familiarising them with a system of planning stories which they can apply to any title. As they work through the units, the children assemble a portfolio of stories containing genre-specific vocabulary and writing features. The chosen text types correspond with those in the Framework's text-level objectives for each half-term.

Each unit also includes information and activities on at least one sentence-level objective. Thus the book also enhances the children's knowledge of grammar, their punctuation and style.

THE PROGRAMME CONTAINS:

a teachers' book comprising:

- notes for teachers on the genres
- copies of exemplar stories together with teaching notes
- guidance on how to develop grammar skills in children's writing
- guidance on how to help children write in the particular genre

a resource book of photocopiable material comprising:

- illustrated versions of the exemplar stories especially produced for children
- notes for the children on understanding the grammar (optional reference material)
- photocopiable activity sheets to reinforce the grammar (optional)
- notes and tips for the children on writing stories (optional reference material)
- differentiated story scaffolds which enable them to choose the course of the story they are about to write
- vocabulary banks for them to use and add to.

HOW TO USE THE PROGRAMME

1 After examining examples of stories in the target genre by established writers, read and discuss the exemplar story with the children, using the notes in the margin to highlight the examples of the unit's grammatical teaching point and writing feature. The children should follow the story using their own illustrated version from the Resource book.

2 Next read through and explain the 'Understanding the grammar and punctuation' section of the unit. The children can do the activities orally together or independently on paper.

3 Then explain the 'Helpful hints' and 'Writing features' sections of the unit to the children.

4 Read through the story scaffolds with the children. Then give them the differentiated word banks and ask them to record their own vocabulary suggestions in the space provided.

Give the children time to plan, write and edit their stories. Each child can then store the best copies of their stories in a writing folder.

NOTES FROM THE AUTHORS

The activities in each unit, from reading the model story to composing a story using the scaffolds, can be used in shared or guided time, with the children working collaboratively or individually.

The order of activities for each unit corresponds exactly with the sequence for the teaching of writing outlined in *Grammar for Writing* (DfEE 0107/2000). First the model story can be discussed and its grammatical and thematic features interrogated during shared reading. Next the grammar and punctuation activities can be undertaken to reinforce the children's understanding of the relevant sentence-level objectives. The helpful hints section, story scaffolds and vocabulary banks support the teacher and children in shared writing sessions and in subsequent guided and independent writing.

The method works well with children of all abilities and with bilingual pupils, as it offers the security of a detailed framework and a bank of appropriate vocabulary together with the challenge of a grammar and writing features component for each unit. As the grammar section contains examples from the story, all the children can access it at some level: it is not always necessary to understand the mechanics of the grammar in order to modify the examples for use in an individual story.

This is the sequence of units for Year 5. The story-type and grammatical information and activities for each unit reflect and fulfil the sentence- and text-level requirements of the NLS Framework for each term.

TERM 1

UNIT 1
Genre: animal stories
Grammar and punctuation component: standard and non-standard English (S2); commas (S6).
Writing feature: presentation of characters through dialogue, action and description (T3).

UNIT 2
Genre: sports stories
Grammar and punctuation component: connectives (S3); punctuating complex sentences (S6).
Writing feature: story beginnings (T1, T11); how characters are presented (T3).

UNIT 3
Genre: magic stories
Grammar and punctuation component: direct and reported speech (S5); setting out and punctuating dialogue (S7).
Writing feature: word play (T8); metaphors and similes (T17).

UNIT 4
Genre: playscripts
Grammar and punctuation component: verbs (S8).
Writing feature: conventions of playscripting (T18).

TERM 2

UNIT 5
Genre: traditional stories – West Indies
Grammar and punctuation component: nouns and pronouns (S10); using punctuation effectively in longer and more complex sentences (S5).
Writing feature: literal and figurative language (T10).

UNIT 6
Genre: science fiction
Grammar and punctuation component: nouns and pronouns (S4); ambiguities in sentence contractions (S7); punctuation to replace intonation, pauses or gestures (S6).
Writing feature: story endings.

UNIT 7
Genre: Irish legends
Grammar and punctuation component: types of sentences; conjunctions; punctuation of complex sentences (S5).
Writing feature: direct speech.

UNIT 8
Genre: Inuit myths
Grammar and punctuation component: constructing sentences (S8); commas in embedding clauses (S9).
Writing feature: heroes and villains (T8).

TERM 3

UNIT 9
Genre: stories from India
Grammar and punctuation component: prepositions (S3); using punctuation marks accurately in complex sentences – dashes and brackets (S4).
Writing feature: features of texts from different cultures (T1).

UNIT 10
Genre: stories in letters
Grammar and punctuation component: paragraphs; apostrophe of possession (S5).
Writing feature: narrative viewpoints (T7).

Animal stories

The term 'animal stories' covers a range of types of stories that incorporate animals. These differences in type usually result from the relationships the animal or animals have in the stories and the position of the narrator.

Animal stories can be about animals relating to each other, without including any relationship to humans, although humans often affect the events in the story, as in *Tarka the Otter*, *Watership Down* or *Animal Farm*. Stories can include a relationship between an animal and humans, as in *Black Beauty*, *White Fang* or *The Snow Goose*. Many of the tales involving animal relationships with humans are portrayed on television and film, such as 'Flipper', 'Champion the Wonder Horse' and 'Free Willy'.

The position of the narrator is important in an animal story. If the narrator is omniscient (all-knowing) then the narrator can 'see' everything that is going on in different places and can 'see' into the minds and feelings of all the characters, whether human or animal. Often, an animal story is told by a first person narration. This provides an insight to the narrator's motive for the relationships within the story.

A hierarchy of needs usually drives the characters in animal stories and the quest to have these needs fulfilled provides the plot. The basic physical needs for food, safety, shelter and freedom from cruelty are added to by the higher order needs for love, understanding and companionship. Relationships are, therefore, very important in an animal story.

The characters often learn something about themselves and change in some way that provides hope for the future. The struggles that ensue in an animal story can mean that a character's life does not always have an obviously happy ending. This is especially true when the needs of the animal or human involved are in competition with each other.

As animals are thought of as more vulnerable than humans, there is a poignancy to the stories that is sometimes lacking in other genres. The powerlessness of the animal is often mirrored in a relationship with a powerless person. Barry Hines has movingly illustrated this in *Kes*. Although this provides the writer with the scope to tap into deeply held emotions, over-sentimentality should be avoided. Many animal stories anthropomorphise animals; that is they ascribe to animals human thoughts, feelings and motives. Although this is entertaining, it should be pointed out to children that we can only guess at what goes on inside an animal from watching their body language as we do not share spoken language with them.

Animal stories teach us about ourselves and our place in the world. They often illustrate our carelessness with each other and the natural world around us. In an ever-increasing urbanisation of our environment and the developing isolation from the natural world through the changes in our lifestyles, animal stories can remind us of much that we have lost.

Animal stories

Examples of animal stories

Woof by Allan Ahlberg (Puffin, 1998)
The Peppermint Pig by Nina Bawden (Puffin, 1998)
Kittens in the Kitchen by Lucy Daniels (Hodder, 1994)
Redwall by Brian Jacques (Red Fox, 1994)
The Sheep Pig by Dick King-Smith (Puffin, 1999)

(For advanced readers)
Watership Down by Richard Adams (Puffin, 1993)
The Incredible Journey by Sheila Burnford (Hodder, 1998)

The children's illustrated version of the story is on page 6 of the resource book.

Fox Hole Inn

Fox Hole Inn stands between two settlements. <u>Sixty years ago,</u>[1] people travelling from one settlement to the other stopped there for food and drink. <u>Travellers, trappers, hunters</u>[2] and those seeking gold in the Great River walked along the track that ran past Fox Hole Inn. Most of them would stay for a night or so. Now, a main road had been built between the settlements and Fox Hole Inn was left behind, a tumbling, semi-derelict sprawl of a building. An old man still lived there. He sometimes came into a settlement for stores, but no one liked him. <u>He walked with a juddering limp that made his bent and bony body sway grotesquely</u>.[3] He also had a nasty temper. People kept out of his way. Sometimes the braver children threw stones at him. <u>He would growl at them like a wild animal</u>.[4]

Kirsty was frightened of him, <u>but she was frightened of many things</u>.[5] She was frightened of her father who shouted at her. <u>She was frightened of losing her mother, who treated her kindly and gently loved her, but looked worn out with care and work</u>.[6] The children in her settlement frightened her because they tormented her for being poor and small and too frightened to talk to anyone.

<u>One day a gang of children followed her, calling her names.</u>[7] Kirsty began to run. She ran and ran, stumbling along the old forest track, the children throwing sticks and making howling noises. She fell over a pothole in the track and gashed her leg. The children gathered round her in a circle, chanting names. She saw someone lifting up a stick to hit her. <u>She closed her eyes waiting for the blow to come.</u>[8] From nowhere the old man appeared, roaring at the children. They ran off, scattering like leaves before a gust of wind. The old man picked her up. "<u>I sawed</u>[9] what they did, <u>the varmints</u>.[10] You'd better come with me and get that knee fixed," he growled. "Fox Hole Inn's just round that bend. Come on".

He grasped her hand and they limped along the track.

Inside Fox Hole Inn, Kirsty sat on an old table, a drink of milk in a dirty glass clenched in her hand. The old man sat down, rolled a cigarette and, glaring at her, drank beer from a cracked mug.

"What're you thinking?" <u>he barked suddenly</u>.[11]

Startled, Kirsty blurted out exactly what she had been thinking.

"I was wondering if <u>you've ever was loved</u>."[12]

He stared at her, put down his mug and said, "You're a scared little thing and that was a brave thing to say. So I'll tell you.

"Once, once I was loved. When I was your age, I had no ma and pa like you've got. I lived here with my aunt and uncle who ran this place. They didn't love me. I got leftover food to eat. I worked for them from the moment the sun <u>rised</u>[13] up over those trees out there to when the last customer had dragged himself drunk to his bed. I slept outside in the shed. I knew nothing of love. The only attention I got was the beatings from my aunt and uncle.

---

1 Comma used after an adverb phrase which begins a sentence.

2 Commas used to separate items in a list.

3 Describing how a character moves can provide an image for the reader. In this case, the movement of the character is a result of the events in the story that unfolds.

4 Reinforcement of the anti social nature of this character.

5 This describes Kirsty's nature at the very beginning of the story. During stories, characters should develop or change in some way as a result of the events.

6 Commas are used to mark off connecting adverbs, adverbial phrases or clauses, in this case to mark off 'who treated her kindly and gently loved her'.

7 Defining a character can also be achieved by how other characters in the story act towards them.

8 This implies that Kirsty is passive and, therefore, a victim.

9 'Saw' is an irregular verb. The old man should have said 'I saw'. It is therefore non-standard English

10 'The varmints' is a form of dialect that is non-standard English now. Using dialects in a story can, however, provide further characterisation. In this case, the intention is to create an old gold rush or early American feel to the story.

11 Using alternative verbs for the characters' actions increases the characterisation and maintains it.

12 Non-standard use of past participle 'loved' following the verb 'to be'. This should read 'you have ever been loved.'

13 Rise is an irregular verb. Here, it has a non-standard form as its past tense is 'rose'.

"Then one day, a vixen and her cub were seen in the clearing that used to be in front of Fox Hole Inn, before those trees out there growed[14] up to its door. A customer got his gun and shot the vixen. She ran, bleeding, into the forest, her cub following closely at her heels. That night, after work, I went in search of the wounded vixen, wondering what had happened to her. I found her lying dead in the forest, her cub whimpering by her side. The fox cub reminded me of myself – young, helpless and scared.[15] The next night I saved my scraps of food and went back to where I'd found him. He had hid[16] in the bushes near his ma's body. I waited, holding out the food. Bit by bit, the frit[17] fox cub crawled out, his body flattened against the forest floor, his whole little frame shook[18] with fear. But I knew that hunger makes critters[19] do things that aren't normal – didn't I put up with everything just to survive myself? The fox cub took the food from my hand and ran back to the bushes.

"Night after night I came with food and water for that little creature. He became braver as time went on. After a while he would come right out of the bushes as I approached. He would sit next to me and eat his food and I would tell him about the hurts and cruel words that made my days. I called him Comfort. He was the only living thing I knowed[20] that was glad to see me or would listen to a word I said.

"Soon every moment I had free I would spend with Comfort. I would use any excuse to go into the forest – collecting sticks for the fire, telling the trappers and hunters I would find animals for them – anything. Whenever I was in the forest, I would call for Comfort and somehow he always found me and came. He began to catch his own food, small birds and rabbits. He often brought me something too. I would light a fire and cook his gift to me. Sometimes we would doze by the fire, his head in my lap.

"As I wandered round the forest doing whatever chores I was supposed to do there, he would follow me. If I stopped to climb a tree, or pick berries, he would sit, his head cocked to one side, as if he was puzzled by my strange behaviour. Comfort, who could be a darn fool, teased me too.[21] He might wander off, then leap out at me from behind a tree, making me jump out of my skin. He would get my trouser leg between his teeth and worry it, pulling me back till I fell over. Then we would play fight, rolling and chasing till we threw ourselves laughing and panting on the forest floor.

"I knew happiness for the first time in my life. The beatings and hardship I knew at Fox Hole Inn never seemed so bad, because my friend was waiting for me in the forest. It was Comfort who taught me to laugh. If I was particularly sad, he always knew and would lean his head against me and lick my hand. Many a night I cried into his coat and I swear his eyes looked at me with understanding.

"One thing Comfort would never do. He would never come near Fox Hole Inn. I would get to a certain tree, five hundred yards from the edge of the clearing and he would turn and disappear into the darkness of the forest. I understood. Fox Hole Inn was a place of dread and terror to us both and there weren't nothing[22] would induce him to come nearer."

The old man took a drag at his cigarette and sighed.

"That day we had the best time ever. It was the dead of winter. Snow lay on the ground two feet deep. There were hardly any customers and my aunt and uncle had gotten real drunk[23] in the morning and were snoring in their beds. I decided to go off for the afternoon with Comfort and put up with the punishment I was sure to get on my return.

14 Grow is an irregular verb. Here, it has a non-standard form as its past tense is 'grew'.

15 This description links the character of the old man as a boy to the fox cub. These characteristics change later in the story as a response to the events.

16 Hide is an irregular verb. Here, it is non-standard as its past tense would be 'hidden'.

17 'Frit' is part of the dialect described in point 10. As such it is non-standard English. Also, its tense should be the past participle, which is 'fritened'.

18 Shake is an irregular verb. Here, it has a non-standard form as the verb 'flattened' is in past participle form and this verb should stay in the same tense, i.e. 'shaken'.

19 'Critters' is part of the dialect used in this story.

20 Know is an irregular verb. To agree with 'was' the standard use would be 'knew'.

21 Commas used around a non-defining clause. A non-defining clause provides information which is not needed to identify the person, thing or group being talked about.

22 'Weren't nothing' is a double negative and as such is non-standard English. (Standard English – 'wasn't anything'.)

23 'Gotten real drunk'. The word 'real' is an adjective being used as an adverb. As such it is non-standard English.

"Comfort and I ran and ran through the silent forest, disturbing the odd bird that rose squawking into the high blue sky. I threw snowballs at Comfort. At first he was startled; then he tried to catch them in his mouth. We tumbled together in the snow, shouting and barking with sheer joy.

"I climbed a tree to shake snow down on Comfort, who jumped and danced underneath, shaking his coat so the snow flew out like exploding jewels. I saw a nest higher up in the tree. In them days, I'm sorry to say, I had stole[24] many a bird's egg to get us something to eat. I began to climb towards it. Comfort whined and yapped at me. I laughed down at him and told him not to be such a baby. I felt so powerful,[25] so free, like I could fly to the treetop. Comfort started to leap up against the tree trunk, yelping, his front paws tearing at the bark. I reached up to grasp the bird's nest. My foot slipped on the branch and I was falling, falling through the black, frozen[26] branches, the face of Comfort rushing towards me as I fell, staring at me with anguish in those tawny brown eyes.

"I thumped to the ground and a searing pain wracked through my leg. I knew it was broken. Comfort licked my face frantically, making little high sounds in his distress. I pushed him away and lifted my head. I could see a piece of bone sticking out of my leg, blood staining the snow around it. Shuddering, I lay my head down again and began to cry. Comfort pushed his head against me; he were[27] trying to make me get up. I shouted at him to stop and he sat down suddenly, surprised because he had never heard me shout like that before. Trembling, I got up onto my elbows and pulled at the tear in my trousers above the wound, thinking I would use a strip of it as a bandage. Comfort came over and got a bit of the material between his teeth and pulled. The pain thundered through my body like an avalanche and I passed out."

The old man stopped his story. With trembling hands[28] he rolled another cigarette and gulped down the rest of his drink. A tear rolled down his face. He wiped his nose with the back of his hand and stared down at the table. Kirsty's heart began to thud.

"What happened?" she whispered.

The old man lifted his head and looked straight at her.

"When I came to I was on a bed back at Fox Hole Inn. The grim, sneering face of my uncle stared down at me from the foot of the bed. A drunk who used to be a doctor[29] was bandaging my leg. When he saw I was conscious he held out a flask of whisky[30] towards me. Something at the back of my mind bothered me. I couldn't work out how I had got to Fox Hole Inn with a broken leg. 'Did I walk back?' I asked, pushing the flask away, though I badly needed the relief from pain I knew the whisky would give me. My uncle and the doctor laughed. Then my uncle leaned over the end of the bed, 'Don't be so stupid. If you hadn't already got a broken leg that'll give you a limp for the rest of your life, I'd give you one myself.'[31]

"The old doctor patted my hand, 'We went out and searched for you, lad. Found you too, thank the Lord. Out cold you have been. Just as well, 'cos it's saved you a deal of pain from being carried back here like a sack of potatoes.' I thought for a moment. 'But how did you know what happened?' I asked. 'Shut them[32] questions snapped my uncle. 'Now, now, the boy's had a shock,' wheezed the doctor.[33] My uncle rubbed the stubble on his chin. 'Lucky for you,' he snarled, 'that we saw a fox with a bit of your trousers in its snout, though dang me if I understand what it was doing with it.'

24 Steal is an irregular verb. After the use of 'had' the past perfect form should be used, i.e. 'stolen'. Therefore, this is non-standard English.

25 This provides a presentation of the character through an internalisation of his feelings. It shows how the events in the story have given a vulnerable character feelings of power, thus developing the character.

26 Commas, used when two or more adjectives are put in front of a noun.

27 Here the subject does not agree with the verb. It is therefore non-standard English. It should read 'he was'.

28 This presents the character's state of mind through action.

29 This is a defining clause. A defining clause gives information that is necessary to identify the person, thing or group being talked about. A pair of commas is not used around a defining clause.

30 This action characterises the doctor. It implies that he is a drunk because he carries a bottle of whisky with him, even in a medical emergency. It also implies that he is unprofessional because he offers whisky to a child.

31 This dialogue from the uncle presents him as a thoroughly nasty piece of work.

32 Using 'them' as a determiner is non-standard English.

33 This dialogue implies that the doctor has maintained some kindliness, although he is decrepit.

"My heart leapt – Comfort! 'Come right up to the door it did,' my uncle continued, 'scratching at it too. <u>I didn't never</u>[34] see a fox behave like that afore. Cheek of the thing, bold as brass, making scratch marks on the door an' all.' I stared at my uncle. <u>Comfort, what was</u>[35] terrified of Fox Hole Inn, had torn off a piece of my trousers and had passed the tree he always stopped at five hundred yards inside the forest. Comfort had crossed the clearing where his mother had been shot. Comfort, gripping my trouser material in his teeth, had, with terror trembling in every limb, gone up to the door of Fox Hole Inn and scratched at it. <u>Comfort had called to these people to save me.</u>[36] Yes, little girl, I have been loved.

"I cried out then, 'Where is he? Where's Comfort now? Please let him come in here; please bring him to me.' They stared at me. 'What are you talking about boy? Has he lost his mind?' my uncle asked the doctor. 'Now, son,' the doctor felt my head, 'quieten down and explain yourself.' I took a deep breath. 'The fox, doctor, please can you bring the <u>fox as came,</u>[37] in here to me? Has he gone back to the forest?' I looked from one to the other. The doctor shook his head. 'He needs a rest. We'd better leave him.' They walked to the door. 'The fox!' I shouted. My uncle turned. 'We shot the ruddy fox. He won't bother you again.' With that my uncle left the room and my world ended. Just like that. Ended."

The room was getting dark now. Kirsty got off the table. She had to get home or she'd be in real trouble.

"I'm sorry," she murmured "I'm so sorry. Thank you for helping me, but I'd better go now."

Kirsty took a deep breath and <u>with more courage than she'd ever felt before</u>[38] said loudly, "<u>I ain't afraid of you no more</u>.[39] I'll come back tomorrow with some of my ma's cakes. I ... I'd like that."

But the old man wasn't listening. He was staring out of the window. Staring at the crowding forest and the black silhouettes of branches that crossed like barbed wire against Fox Hole Inn.

34 'I didn't never' is a double negative and so it is non-standard English.

35 Using 'what' as a relative pronoun is non-standard English.

36 The character Comfort has overcome his fears through his love of the child. The events in the story have caused Comfort to change from the 'young, helpless and scared' description provided at the beginning of the story.

37 Using 'as' as a relative pronoun is non-standard English.

38 Kirsty has changed through the kindness of the old man and through listening to his story.

39 This is a double negative and so it is non-standard English. 'Ain't' is non-standard English for 'I'm not'.

Understanding the grammar and punctuation

Grammar pointers

Standard and non-standard English

It is important when discussing standard and non-standard English that the discussion is based on the words 'standard' and 'non-standard' as opposed to 'right' and 'wrong' as this could cause feelings of resentment in children and their parents who speak or write using non-standard English.

Non-standard English is usually created by use of the following:

- Non-standard formation of the past tense in irregular verbs. A regular verb will end in 'ed' in the past tense. An irregular verb will not.

  I sawed what they did.

  'See' is an irregular verb. The standard use would be *I saw what they did.*

- Non-standard agreement between the subject and the verb.

  He were trying to make me get up.

  Standard formation of the past tense of 'to be' is:

  Singular: *I was, you were, he/she/it was*
  Plural: *We were, you were, they were*

- Non-standard use of adjectives as adverbs.

  There were hardly any customers and my aunt and uncle had gotten real drunk.

  'Real' in standard English, is an adjective, as it describes nouns; for example a 'real' drink. The word 'drunk' is an adjective in the above sentence and the adverb 'real' describes the adjective.

- Using 'them' as a determiner.

  'Shut them questions,' snapped my uncle.

  A determiner is put at the beginning of a noun group to distinguish what you are talking about, such as 'the', 'these', 'those' and 'that'. 'Them' is not used as a determiner in standard English.

- Using double negatives.

  Fox Hole Inn was a place of dread and terror to us both and there weren't nothing would induce him to come nearer.

- Using 'what' or 'as' as a relative pronoun.

  Comfort, what was terrified of Fox Hole Inn...

  Relative pronouns refer to something that has already been mentioned. In standard English, relative pronouns are: who, whom, which or that.

'Non-standard English' is a term that also describes some uses of language in dialects that would not be used as 'standard'.

Punctuation Pointers

Commas

- Commas are used to separate items in lists. They are also used after an adverb phrase that begins a sentence.

  Sixty years ago, people travelling from one settlement to the other stopped there for food and drink.

  'Sixty years ago' is an adverb phrase.

- Commas are also used to mark off connecting adverbs and adverbial or relative clauses.

  She was frightened of losing her mother, who treated her kindly and loved her, but looked worn out...

  'Who treated her kindly and gently loved her' is an adverbial clause.

- Commas are used when two adjectives are put in front of a noun.

  the black, frozen branches

> The children's version of these notes is
> on page 11 of the resource book.

Writing features
Presenting characters through dialogue, action and description

Although dialogue, action and description are interlinked in creating written characters, each of these can be taught separately to begin with, before the children put them together in a piece of writing.

When writing characters, it is important for the children to understand two main criteria. The first is that a well written main character will develop in some way during the story. This could mean that the character learns something, changes their mind, gains skills or begins a new way of life as a result of their experiences in the story. In 'Fox Hole Inn', the old man had learned to be disaffected by his isolation from others, but has maintained his caring attitude towards victims. It is implied at the end of the story that a possible new friendship with Kirsty might break through his defences.

Although the main character will change or develop, their basic characteristics should be maintained throughout the story. For example, if the main character begins the story speaking in a dialect, this dialect must be maintained. If the main character is a rough-and-ready sort of person, they may learn how to be more gentle, but their dialogue and actions will still demonstrate a certain roughness. Kirsty finds courage at the end of the story in 'Fox Hole Inn', but she still maintains a timidity in her speech patterns.

The second is that characters should interact in a meaningful way. This could simply mean that the main character responds to how other characters in the story speak or act. It could mean that the character takes a course of action in response to other characters, but this must be made explicit in the story. The interaction between Kirsty and the old man provides Kirsty with the courage to say "I was wondering if you've ever was loved?" which provokes the old man into telling her the story, but he provides his reason for telling her by saying "That was a brave thing to say. So I'll tell you." Some idea of how other characters make the main character feel or vice versa is a useful device, but should be treated delicately in a short story. A phrase or two should be sufficient. For example, the old man relates his feelings towards the fox cub by saying "I knew happiness for the first time in my life."

Dialogue

Everyone has their own particular speech patterns. These could include certain phrases, tones of voice, dialect and so on. Characters in stories can be implied through their own personal speech patterns, how others respond verbally to them and through the interaction between them. In 'Fox Hole Inn' the old man's uncle uses phrases such as "Don't be so stupid," and "Shut them questions." which show him to be a particularly nasty, unsympathetic character. Using other verbs for 'said' is a useful skill to ask the children to try. Characters in 'Fox Hole Inn' provide some alternatives that indicate their personalities. These include:

> *growl, roaring, barked, blurted out, call, cried, sighed, shouting, whined, yapped, whispered, snapped, wheezed*

The children could be asked which of the above belong to characters in the story.

Action

The use of powerful verbs is one of the most important aspects of creating characters in stories. Providing mannerisms that fit the character is a strong device for implying character. The children could be asked to discuss people they know or have seen and to describe the way they move. The old man 'walked with a juddering limp that made his bent and bony body sway grotesquely,' whereas Kirsty runs, falls over and sits still throughout the story. Providing contrasts between characters in this way enhances the interest in the story.

Action can also imply how the characters are feeling. On the day of the accident in 'Fox Hole Inn', the joy felt by the old man at his freedom and friendship with the fox described through the actions they take – running, throwing snowballs, tumbling and so on.

Description

Adverbs, adjectives, similes and metaphors are the main tools of description. These need to be used precisely as sometimes children get carried away and will provide long lists of adjectives or inappropriate metaphors and similes in their descriptions. Adverbs can enhance the characterisation of the action of a character. Adjectives can not only provide an explanation of how a character looks, but also how that character feels and the sort of objects in the character's world and how they appear to the character. Similes and metaphors extend this.

> There are helpful hints for children writing an animal story on page 14 of the resource book.

Sports stories

Writers of sports stories entertain their readers not merely by showing some knowledge or interest in the particular sport written about in their story, but also in using this as a backdrop against which their characters overcome some personal challenge or obstacle.

In sports stories, a strong opening is essential, with the setting and characters introduced as early as possible in order that the story can move forward at an appropriate pace.

Sports stories are quite often similar to adventure stories in that there is a strong element of action taking place. The use of connectives that signal time, such as 'early that morning' or 'later that day' can help to move the action along, as can descriptions of what/how/where action is taking place.

A certain amount of technical knowledge and sporting terminology is useful but the children need not rely wholly upon this. The vocabulary needed to describe the action taking place can be quite simple and, used at appropriate places in the story, will enable the children to create believable events rather than overloading their writing with technical terms.

Sports stories

Examples of sports stories

The Goalkeeper's Revenge by Bill Naughton (Puffin, 1999)

FA Cup Mini Series by Haydn Middleton (Scholastic, 1999):
Come and have a go if you think you're SMART enough
Come and have a go if you think you're COOL enough
Come and have a go if you think you're MAD enough
Come and have a go if you think you're RICH enough

Here We Go by Diane Redmond (Yearling, 1994)
Foul by Paul Cockburn (Virgin, 1996)
Football Mad by Paul Stewart (Scholastic, 1997)
Cliffhanger by Jacqueline Wilson (Corgi Yearling Books, 2000)
Riding the Waves by Theresa Tomlinson (Walker Books, 2001)
A Horse by Any Other Name by Jenny Hughes (The Kenilworth Press, 1996)
A Horse For the Summer by Michelle Bates (Usborne Publishing, 1996)

The children's illustrated version of the story is on page 21 of the resource book.

Teamwork[1]

"So, the charity fund-raising event this year," boomed the voice of the head teacher, Mrs Grant, "will be a football match between the Year 6 and Year 5 teams."[2]

There was a cheer from the back of the hall as[3] the Year 5 boys heard those words. Usually, the charity event was for Year 6 only. Ben Shearer and Alex Fraser beamed at each other. They both knew that Year 5 had by far the better team and the better chance of winning since Ben was the best goalie in the school and Alex had a strong reputation for his scoring abilities. Besides,[4] Year 6 had lost most of their matches against other schools this season.[5]

Ben and Alex felt an air of certainty about the impending match as they discussed it on their walk home after school.

"Fancy a practice before tea?" Ben suggested.

"Good idea," agreed Alex as the two boys ran excitedly up their neighbouring paths, dropping schoolbags, muddy PE kits and football boots in hallways, each making their way towards kitchen snacks.[6]

"That sounds like a great idea," Mrs Fraser encouraged. "Will parents be invited?"

"Think so," muttered Alex, his mouth full of fruit cake. "Mrs Grant says we're getting proper tickets printed and everything."

Ben and Alex had grown up together. Since they were babies, they had been next-door neighbours: sharing toys; going to the park and playgroup together; starting school together; and, more recently,[7] joining the local junior football team together. Ben was a natural in goal and was coached and encouraged by his father.[8] Alex followed in his older brother's footsteps; he was a striker for a league team. Thanks to the two boys, the Cholsey Junior Football Team had won an enviable collection of trophies and shields.

The date for the charity match was announced in the next school assembly. It would be the Saturday before half-term week, which gave teams, coaches, staff and the PTA just three weeks to organise and prepare. Letters were given out requesting help in selling tickets, refreshments, advertising, alerting local papers … the whole school would be involved in various ways. As the days passed[9] and the training sessions became more intense, so the excitement grew and grew.

"What d'you think the score's going to be?" Alex asked Ben during the journey home after a long and wearying training session.

"Mmm, three–nil to us," grinned Ben.

Alex gaped. "Only three?"

Ben nudged him. "Kidding!"

1. The title implies a sports story but the reader needs to read on to find out more and to find out which sport is being written about.

2. The story begins with dialogue, taking the reader straight into the action of the story. This helps to gain the reader's attention.

3. The word 'as' is a conjunction which is one type of connective found in this story.

4. 'Besides' is a connecting adverb, another type of connective, which is used here for emphasis. It is immediately followed by a comma.

5. The setting and characters are introduced early in order to move the story on at a good pace.

6. Commas to separate items in a list.

7. A colon and semicolons are used in addition to commas in this complex sentence in order to separate the listed phrases without losing the flow of information.

8. Character description that provides an insight for the reader.

9. Connective to show the passing of time.

"More like ten–nil," shouted Alex, dodging Ben's schoolbag, "and that's only if **you**[10] don't let any in!"[11]

The two boys shouted and cajoled each other until they reached home, exhausted.

"Never underestimate the opposition," Mr Shearer told Ben seriously as they sat down to eat that evening. "From what I've heard, Mr Cole is giving Year 6 some extra coaching, so you might have to be on your toes!"

Ben told Alex what his father had said as they sat by the goalpost after their evening practice.

"D'you think Mr Cole wants Year 6 to win?" asked Ben. "He's supposed to be **our** class teacher!"

"Nah!" replied Alex, having pondered the question for a moment. "They need all the help they can get. That Max can't score for toffee!!"

"What if we lose…?" Ben began, then stopped as he realised Alex was up and about to take a penalty kick.[12] Ben took up his position, leapt into the air and caught the ball Alex had swiftly booted towards the goalmouth.

"See?" said Alex. "Nothing to worry about."[13]

The next few days[14] at school were busy: posters were designed to go in shop windows around the town; banners were made to cheer on the Year 5 and Year 6 teams; coloured streamers were created and everyone took home books of tickets to sell to family, friends and neighbours.[15] No one in town could escape Cholsey Primary School's charity event this year.

The last training session was on Friday afternoon and suddenly, for some reason, Alex began to feel butterflies in his stomach. Nerves were not something Alex usually suffered from before a match, but today was different.[16] Something wasn't going right. Out on the pitch, he practised his tackles, his passes and his ball-control. Although everything went like clockwork, he had an uneasy feeling and couldn't explain why. He wouldn't mention it to Ben in case he thought he was daft.[17]

Finally,[18] the day of the Cholsey Charity Match arrived. At half past two, the teams assembled in their classrooms, ready to change into strips donated by two local, rival sports shops.[19] Much to Alex and Ben's delight, their strip was red, the same colour as Alex's brother's team. Year 6 would play in blue.

"Cool," said Ben, admiringly as Alex adjusted his collar and ran just a tiny amount of gel through his hair. Just then, Mr Cole arrived at the classroom door, looking a little ruffled.

"Er…, we have a little problem."

Alex and Ben exchanged glances as Mr Cole fiddled with his watchstrap.

"Bit of a crisis, I'm afraid. Year 6 are a player short due to an unexpected injury. Max fell off his bike on his way here and it seems he's broken his leg."

Alex looked heavenwards. Max had a reputation for being accident-prone. Mr Cole continued, "Consequently, as both subs[20] are ill with flu we'll need to 'borrow' one of you … any volunteers?"

10 The word is written in bold to emphasise it.

11 This dialogue reveals the good relationship between the two characters.

12 Use of a technical term.

13 Ending a section with dialogue creates an interesting 'hook' and, in the same way as the opening, invites the reader to read on.

14 The passing of time.

15 A colon is used to announce a list and semicolons are used to separate complicated items in a list.

16 This sentence begins with a coordinate clause, separated from the second main clause by a comma.

17 This description provides the reader with an insight into the character's personality.

18 Connective of time.

19 The opening phrase here indicates time and reminds the reader of the players' sense of anxiety and excitement about the impending match.

20 Technical term.

The team shuffled, heads down, saying nothing.

"In that case," sighed Mr Cole, "we'll have to draw out a number at random."

The room fell silent.[21] Mr Cole quickly wrote the team's numbers on separate pieces of paper and placed them inside his baseball cap. Ben was the exception. Mr Cole offered Ben the hat and told him to pick out just one. Ben knew better than to argue with Mr Cole. The team exchanged anxious glances, muttering, "Not me," and "No way," whilst Ben fiddled nervously with the folded papers before finally pulling one out and giving it to Mr Cole.

Slowly, Mr Cole unfolded the paper and announced the player who would 'defect' to the Year 6 team for this important match.

"Sorry, Alex, luck of the draw I'm afraid," Mr Cole said as he handed Alex the blue shirt. Alex felt a rush of panic and tears began to prick his eyes but he managed to fight them back. He couldn't look his team-mates in the eye, least of all Ben, and simply allowed himself to be ushered out of the classroom towards the waiting Year 6 team.

A huge roar went up as the teams poured out onto the pitch.[22] Mrs Grant welcomed the spectators, said a few words about the proceeds from the event, then the coin was flipped and ends were chosen. The referee blew the whistle and the game began. Alex felt as if he was in a dream. Again and again, he made controlled passes, blocked tackles and worked mechanically, but his heart wasn't in it because he was terrified of having to face Ben.

At half-time, the score was nil–nil.[23] The game continued without Alex's usual air of self-confidence and enthusiasm. Then, with two minutes to go, Jack, captain of the Year 6 team, passed the ball to Abigail, who swiftly took it down the wing towards Alex. This couldn't be happening. What was he supposed to do if he got the ball? Ben knew all of Alex's tactics and vice versa but they'd **never** played on opposing teams before. And then a penalty was awarded to Year 6. Jack gestured to Alex to take it. Everyone knew this was Alex's strong point. Taking a deep breath, Alex focused before running towards the ball. It soared high but Ben's fingers touched it, almost deflecting it. Suddenly, the ball seemed to change direction, curved over Ben's arm and into the goal mouth.[24] The spectators cheered. Year 6 ran over to Alex and slapped him on the back. The final whistle blew. It was over. Year 6 had won one nil. Alex hung his head as he walked slowly back to the classroom but he needn't have worried. Ben was waiting, holding out the red shirt Alex should have worn.

"Well played, mate," he beamed.

"Fancy a practice later?" asked Alex, nervously.

"You bet," grinned his friend.[25]

21 The short sentence emphasises the shock felt by the characters in the story.

22 This sentence sets the mood for the description of the match. It helps to build up the excitement.

23 The opening phrase here indicates time being an important factor.

24 'Suddenly' is a connecting adverb which suggests intensity and quickens the pace.

25 Dialogue ends the story. Having dialogue at the beginning and end gives the story shape.

Understanding the grammar and punctuation

Understanding the grammar and punctuation enables children to control the language they use and therefore to write more interesting and powerful stories.

Grammar pointers

Help the children to be aware of the following when writing their sports stories:

Complex sentences

A complex sentence contains a main clause, which can stand alone as a simple sentence, and one or more subordinate clauses, whose meaning is dependent on the main clause. Links between the main and subordinate clauses are often made by the use of connectives. Words such as *although*, *however*, *if* and *unless* pave the way for the subordinate clause to follow.

Connectives

Connectives are words and phrases that help bring cohesion to a text by creating links between ideas in nearby sentences. Connectives can turn a series of short, simple sentences into more complex and interesting sentences, reducing the disjointed, staccato effect of too many short sentences in a text. Connectives can be conjunctions (*but, when, because, as*) or connecting adverbs (*however, then, therefore*). Some of the most common connectives are:

   also, furthermore, moreover
(to show addition)

   however, nevertheless, on the other hand
(to show opposition)

   besides, anyway, after all
(for emphasis; to strengthen an idea)

   for example, in other words, that is to say
(for explanation and clarification)

   first(ly), first of all, finally
(to show a sequence)

   therefore, consequently, as a result
(to show an outcome or result)

   just then, suddenly, later, meanwhile, next, eventually
(to show the passing of time)

Punctuation pointers

Commas

Commas can be used to separate items in a list. (If the items in that list are long, then a semicolon is used.) It is not usual to place a comma before the 'and'. For example:

   ...dropping schoolbags, muddy PE kits and football boots in hallways...

When sentences start with a subordinate clause, the clauses are separated by commas. However, the children need to be aware that depending on where they place a comma, the meaning of the sentence may be changed.

The comma is used immediately after many connecting adverbs; such as anyway, finally, meanwhile and nevertheless. For example:

   Besides, Year 6 had lost most of their matches against other schools this season.

The colon

The colon is used to announce something that comes next in a sentence. This could be speech; a list; a quotation; or an idea, explanation or consequence. For example:

   The next few days at school were busy: posters were designed to go in shop windows around the town; banners were made to cheer on the Year 5 and Year 6 teams; coloured streamers were created and everyone took home books of tickets to sell to family, friends and neighbours.

The semicolon

A semicolon can be used instead of a conjunction to indicate that two clauses in a sentence are very closely related. It can be used to contrast two ideas in a sentence and it can also be used to separate items in a complicated list (as in the previous example above).

The children's version of these notes is on page 25 of the resource book.

Writing features
Story openings and creating characters

Story openings

Explain to the children that there is a variety of ways in which they can open their stories, depending on the mood they wish to create.

For example, a story can begin with:

1 Dialogue:
   "So, the charity fund-raising event this year," boomed the voice of the head teacher, Mrs Grant, "will be a football match between the Year 6 and Year 5 teams."

2 An interesting sentence that takes the reader straight into the action or setting:
   It was the most frightening thing that Jane had ever seen in her entire life.

3 A question:
   Who would have thought that a day which had begun so normally would end so strangely?

4 A question addressed to the reader:
   If I told you what happened to me that day, you wouldn't believe me, would you?

5 An exclamation:
   Sam could not believe her luck!

6 A description:
   The moon shone eerily onto the lake, creating shimmering ripples that reflected the dark, menacing branches of the overhanging trees.

7 The introduction of the characters:
   Ginger was the strangest boy in the class.

Emphasise to the children that their story opening should invite the reader to read on and find out more about the action/adventure to be unfolded and discuss the most appropriate openings for a sports story.

Creating characters

There are several ways that an author can present a character's personality in a story.

1 Description:
   The writer describes an aspect of the appearance, personality or personal history of the character.

   Ben was a natural in goal and was coached and encouraged by his father.

2 Dialogue:
   The words that the characters speak, or the comments of a first person narrator, reveal their thoughts, their feelings and the motives for their actions. Conversations between characters show the reader how they relate to one another.

   "What d'you think the score's going to be?"
   "Mmm, three nil to us," grinned Ben,
   Alex gaped. "Only three?"
   Ben nudged him. "Kidding!"
   *"More like ten nil," shouted Alex, dodging Ben's schoolbag, "and that's only if **you** don't let any in!"*

3 Action:
   The behaviour of the characters also provides the reader with more information and helps to make them 'rounded' or real.

   Alex began to feel butterflies in his stomach. Nerves were not something Alex usually suffered from before a match, but today was different.

There are helpful hints for children on writing a sports story on page 28 of the resource book.

Magic stories

In magic stories, the main character is usually an ordinary person who either suddenly discovers hidden powers or is drawn into an extraordinary situation. Often, there are magical beings, animals or strange places in magic stories that contrast with the ordinary world.

Magic and fantasy stories can encapsulate a combination of imaginary places, mythological beings, supernatural forces and extraordinary powers and abilities. There is often a dream-like or fairytale quality to the setting, such as enchanted forests and medieval castles, although modern-day inventions such as computers can be used to create magical and fantastic adventures.

We also find in many magic stories the customary witch, wizard or goblin, with talking animals, objects possessing strange powers and the main character's ability to fly, become invisible or turn people into animals.

Almost always, there is a contrast between good and bad in some form. At least one character will represent the 'dark side' and the main character usually has to find ways of escaping from or overcoming these evil powers.

Magic and fantasy stories are similar in that they can be written in a light-hearted or sinister vein, depending on whether the purpose is to amuse, entertain or terrify the reader!

The magical worlds created in this genre are often parallel in some way to real life, although the powers used to overcome difficulties are superhuman, supernatural and often incredible.

Magic stories

Examples of magic stories

Harry Potter and the Philosopher's Stone by J K Rowling (Bloomsbury Children's Books, 1997)
Harry Potter and the Chamber of Secrets by J K Rowling (Bloomsbury Children's Books, 1999)
Harry Potter and the Goblet of Fire by J K Rowling (Bloomsbury Children's Books, 2000)
Harry Potter and the Prisoner of Azkaban by J K Rowling (Bloomsbury Children's Books, 2001)
Harry Potter and the Order of the Phoenix by J K Rowling (Bloomsbury Children's Books, 2003)

The Worst Witch by Jill Murphy (Puffin, 1982)
The Worst Witch Strikes Again by Jill Murphy (Puffin, 1993)
The Worst Witch All at Sea by Jill Murphy (Puffin, 2000)

The Chronicles of Narnia by C S Lewis (Collins, 1970)

(For advanced readers)

The Weirdstone of Brisingamen by Alan Garner (Collins, 1981)
The Owl Service by Alan Garner (Collins, 1979)
Elidor by Alan Garner (Collins, 1981)
The Hobbit by J R R Tolkien (Collins, 1973)

The children's illustrated version of the story is on page 35 of the resource book.

The Witch of Class 5B

"Right, everyone! Quiet!" called Mrs Broome, clapping her hands briskly. "David and Megan, whatever is the matter now?"[1]

As usual, 5B were taking longer than any other class in the school to settle for afternoon registration. As usual, David and Megan were having another of their disagreements.

"You can't even spell,"[2] David mocked, holding up the animal poster Megan had been working on in Literacy.

"Yes I can," hissed[3] Megan, trying to snatch the poster from David's taunting grasp.

"Enough!" shouted Mrs Broome over the noise. David obligingly gave Megan back her poster and sat down.

"That hurt!" yelped Megan as David sneakily prodded her with a freshly-sharpened pencil just as Mrs Broome turned to open the register.

"That does it!" Mrs Broome exploded. "Megan, you come and sit next to Zoe. David, put the pencil down. Down!" Mrs Broome sighed, tidied the bun at the back of her head and adjusted her glasses. "That's better," she said, calmly.[4]

Wednesday afternoons were always like this. On Wednesday afternoons, 5B had science and the current topic was the life-cycle of the frog. The class had already collected frogspawn from the school's nature garden and watched daily as the tadpoles began to grow and develop. Today, they had to work in groups, drawing the stages of development.

"I'd like you all to write a sentence underneath each picture, describing each stage of the frog's life," Mrs Broome explained, scanning the class with her razor eyes.[5]

Megan glared at David who sneered back.[6] "Hmmph, I wish I could turn David Jackson into a frog," Megan muttered quietly.

As quick as a flash,[7] Mrs Broome turned around from the whiteboard and pointed her marker pen at Megan with a steel gaze. "Megan Brown, shame on you!" was all she said.

Megan looked around, puzzled and embarrassed. She hadn't said it so that anyone near her could hear, so how on earth could Mrs Broome?

Megan sucked her pen, thinking hard. The more she thought, the more she could visualise nasty, ugly David as a frog. He stuck his tongue out at her and she imagined him sitting by a pond, catching flies with his long, sticky frog tongue.

At home, Megan daydreamed about turning David into a frog. She was still thinking about it as she fed Oscar.

"Only witches can turn people into frogs," Megan complained, stroking Oscar's soft, coal-black fur as he ate and purred simultaneously, "and

---

1 Direct speech takes the reader straight into the story and introduces the characters. We are immediately informed that the characters David and Megan do not get on.

2 The word 'spell' is a pun. The reader will discover the significance of this as the story unfolds.

3 The word 'hissed' tells us how angry the character is feeling.

4 Direct speech where there are several sentences interrupted by narrative. Each sentence begins with a capital letter.

5 'her razor eyes' describes Mrs Broome's penetrating stare and is metaphorical.

6 In just a few words, the author tells us how the characters are reacting to each other.

7 'As quick as a flash' is a familiar simile.

witches have familiars. Did you know that, Oscar?"[8]

"Of course," the cat replied, looking up from his bowl. He raised an eyebrow.[9]

Megan, who was heading for the kitchen door, stopped in her tracks. She spun around like lightning.[10]

"Oscar …. you can speak!"

The cat sighed, "Naturally. I am your familiar and you … are a witch."[11]

Megan gasped and asked Oscar how she could possibly be a witch.

"Humans!" tutted Oscar. "All the females in your family are witches, my dear. Now … who is it you want to turn into a frog?"

Oscar listened patiently as Megan told him all about David Jackson and his mean ways. The cat twitched his whiskers.[12]

"Very well. I'll help," he said, "but you must remember that magic is a serious business, not to be entered into lightly. Are you sure you're up to it?"

Megan thought for a moment.

"Definitely," she nodded. "I want to get back at that David Jackson!"

"In that case," the cat considered, "we will need a spell."

It took until bedtime, but at last they had devised a spell just right for turning a boy into a frog.

At school the next morning, Megan breezed into the classroom and took her place next to David. He scowled at her, ready to snatch her pencil case and empty the contents onto the table, a ritual he performed every morning. Megan didn't flinch. She remained as cool as a cucumber,[13] retrieving the scattered items and replacing them neatly in her pink, fluffy pencil case. David was puzzled. Normally, she retaliated with teeth and nails and hair flying, but not today. He wondered why.[14]

After assembly, Mrs Broome began the Literacy session.

"This morning, I'd like you to write a poem," she explained, "about an animal of your choice, describing it without actually naming it."

The girls immediately went into raptures about their pet hamsters, rabbits, dogs and ponies. The boys asked if they could write about unusual pets like snakes and spiders.

"Why can't we do a poem about football or something?" David whined.

"David," Mrs Broome retorted sharply, "we have read 'Animal Poems' together in class. Were you too busy being a nuisance to listen?"

David turned red as the rest of his table sniggered.[15]

Megan had already decided on her animal and completed her poem, decorated a border around it and handed it to Mrs Broome before anyone else. Now, she had nothing to do.

8   In the first sentence, the direct speech is interrupted by narrative. Therefore, the speech is reopened with a lower-case letter.

9   Talking animals are a common feature of the magical/fantasy genre.

10 An example of a simile.

11 An example of dialogue at the end of a sentence.

12 This type of reported speech allows the narrative to flow without becoming burdened with too much detail.

13 'As cool as a cucumber' is another familiar simile, used to describe Megan's confidence.

14 This helps to build up the anticipation of what is to come.

15 'read' and 'red' is a play on words.

"Mrs Broome, could I please go to the nature garden?" she asked, tentatively.

Mrs Broome looked at her over the top of her glasses and nodded without saying anything.

At break, Mrs Broome gave Megan a sticker for her poem and smiled before heading off to the staff room for her coffee. Megan quickly snatched up her poem and ran outside. David was walking towards the nature garden with a large stick in his hand, no doubt intent on doing some damage. There wasn't a moment to lose.

"Oh no you don't, David Jackson," Megan whispered, crouching behind a bush. She opened her book and began to read:
>Cold, slimy skin,
>Boggly-eyed and dim,
>Hopping from stone to stone.
>Long sticky tongue
>Jump in this pond
>And leave us all alone.

Megan looked up. David was nowhere to be seen. In his place was a large, fat frog with green, leathery skin, looking rather bewildered. It had worked.

<u>"There," said Megan to the frog, "and you said I couldn't spell!"</u>[16]

"Very good, Megan." The voice behind her startled Megan and she turned as white as a sheet when she saw Mrs Broome standing there. "However, I think we should turn David back into his boy shape. I'm sure he'll turn over a new leaf now."

"But …" Megan began.

"Leave it to me," Mrs Broome said briskly. She muttered some strange words and a few seconds later, David was standing where the frog had been, looking shaken but none the worse for his adventure. Mrs Broome pointed her marker pen at him and stared at him intently. "David Jackson, you will never misbehave in class again."

David nodded sheepishly and ran off to the playground. Megan couldn't believe what she had seen.

<u>"Mrs Broome, you're a …"</u>

<u>"… witch. Yes that's right," Mrs Broome</u>[17] said, "but don't let anyone know, will you?"

Megan shook her head, speechless.

"There's just one more thing, Megan," Mrs Broome said, sternly. "We really only have room for one witch in 5B, so no more magic in school. Agreed?" Her expression softened.

"Agreed," nodded Megan, feeling very relieved.

Oscar, who had been watching from the fence, turned to go home.

"Humans!" he tutted in despair.

16 The significance of the word 'spell' is apparent here.

17 The reader now realises that Mrs Broome's name is also a play on words.

Understanding the grammar and punctuation

Understanding the grammar and punctuation enables children to control the language they use and therefore to write more interesting and powerful stories.

Grammar pointers

Direct and reported speech

Direct speech is the words actually spoken by a character in the story (or anybody else whose speech the author needs to record) and is enclosed in inverted commas (speech or quotation marks).

"Right, everyone! Quiet!" called Mrs Broome.

Reported speech is where the author reports what was said without using the actual words the speaker said.

Megan gasped and asked Oscar how she could possibly be a witch.

Help the children to understand that using a mixture of direct and reported speech in their writing will give it variety. If long stretches of direct speech are used, the reader can become bored or lose track of who is speaking. Used sparingly, direct speech can have much greater impact.

Direct speech can tell the reader a lot about a character but the disadvantage is that it can slow down the pace of narrative. Help the children to consider whether some of their dialogue could be changed to reported speech to avoid this pitfall.

Reported speech can be useful for:
+ providing a contrast between what a character actually says and what he or she is thinking;
+ summarising what a character says without interrupting the flow of the narrative.

Punctuation pointers

Setting out and punctuating dialogue

Explain to the children that when setting out dialogue it is important to give each new speaker a new line in order to avoid confusion about who is speaking. Direct speech must be enclosed in speech marks, separated from the reporting clause (narrative) with appropriate punctuation (ie comma, question mark or exclamation mark).

"That does it!" Mrs Broome exploded. "Megan, you come and sit next to Zoe. David, put the pencil down. Down!"

Explain that, in the above speech, a new line is not needed for Mrs Broome's second sentence as the speaker has not changed.

There are four types of direct speech:

1. speech at the beginning of the sentence;

    "You can't even spell," David mocked...

Point out to the children that a comma, question mark or exclamation mark precedes the closing speech mark.

2. speech at the end of the sentence;

    The cat sighed, "Naturally. I am your familiar and you ... are a witch."

Highlight the comma that precedes the opening speech mark. Explain to the children that the first word of the direct speech begins with a capital letter as it is the first word of the sentence of the speech.

3. a single sentence of dialogue interrupted by narrative;

    "In that case," the cat considered, "we will need a spell."

Show the children how the example above is actually one sentence separated by narrative and therefore commas are used to separate the speech from the rest of the sentence. They precede the closing speech mark at the end of the first part of speech and the opening speech mark before the second part of the speech. The second part does not begin with a capital letter because it is a continuation of the sentence.

4. two or more sentences of dialogue separated by narrative.

    "That does it!" Mrs Broome exploded. "Megan, you come and sit next to Zoe. David, put the pencil down. Down!"

The direct speech is separate sentences so there is a capital letter and full stop (or exclamation mark) for each.

The children's version of these notes is on page 39 of the resource book.

Writing features
Word play, metaphors and similes

Word play

A pun is a play on words that can create a humorous or ironic effect. Puns can use words that have double meanings, for example:

spell = magic spell
= to put the correct letters in the right order to make a word

Puns can also use words that sound the same but are spelled differently and have different meanings, for example:

"... we have <u>read</u> 'Animal Poems' together ..."

David turned <u>red</u>.

Encourage the children to make a list of puns they could use in their own stories.

The teacher in the story has an appropriate name for a witch (Mrs Broome). This is also a play on words.

Similes and metaphors

Similes and metaphors are examples of figurative language through which writers express vivid images by the use of comparison.

A simile is identified by its use of 'as' or 'like' in making a comparison.

As quick as a flash, Mrs Broome turned around from the whiteboard ...

She spun around like lightning.

She remained as cool as a cucumber ...

A metaphor allows the writer to liken one thing to another by stating that something actually is something else.

"I'd like you all to write a sentence underneath each picture, describing each stage of the frog's life," Mrs Broome explained, scanning the class with her razor eyes.

Here the character's eyes are called razor eyes to tell the reader how sharp they were.

The children should be encouraged to make up their own similes and metaphors in their stories but the following list can be used to give some ideas:

as black as thunder

as black as coal

as white as a ghost

as white as a sheet

as clean as a whistle

as quick as a flash

as cool as a cucumber

as brave as a lion

as cunning as a fox

as stubborn as a mule

as strong as an ox

as heavy as lead

as light as a feather

The giant's voice was thunder.

The girl's eyes were diamonds in a dark sky.

His steel eyes pierced her gaze.

The demon car raced away.

She sat there, a tigress about to pounce.

His boss was a bullfrog, big and bloated.

The cat was a lion, devouring its prey.

There are helpful hints for children for writing a magic story on page 42 of the Resource book.

Playscripts

A playscript is a narrative that has been written for a dramatic performance. Playscripts usually conform to the basic conventions of storytelling but playwrights do not have the same freedom with structure that story writers have. The work is often organised into large sections called 'Acts' within which there are several smaller sections called 'Scenes'. Unlike the story writer, a playwright has few descriptive tools at his disposal; he needs to establish the characters entirely through what they say and do or by what other characters say about them. The playwright, does, however, have other tools to bring the story alive, namely the sets, costumes, lighting and sound.

As in stories, the plot needs to be strong to maintain interest – the audience's attention needs to be maintained. This is usually achieved by making sure the individual scenes within the play end on an exciting note. The ending of the play is vital to its success. The audience needs to be satisfied that the characters' problems and adventures have come to a satisfactory conclusion – there needs to be a 'feel-good' factor at the end of the play.

Children should be given practice in reading plays. They have to learn about the conventions of playscripting in order to understand which parts of the text are read aloud and which parts are written as stage directions.

They need a lot of experience in writing effective narratives before they can succeed at writing plays. They should be aware of the importance of developing the characters and the plot so as not to get carried away with just writing the dialogue!

For information about the conventions of playscript layout refer to page 32.

Playscripts

Examples of playscripts

Lower ability: *Playtales, Hansel and Gretel* by Moira Butterfield (Heinemann, 1997)

Roald Dahl's 'Charlie and the Chocolate Factory' adapted by Richard George (Puffin Books, 1979)

The Christmas Story by David Wood, illustrated by Asun Balzola (A&C Black Ltd, 1996)

Cheer and Groan by John Townsend (Hutchinson and Co. Ltd, 1985)

Meg and Mog based on books by Helen Nicoll and Jan Pienkowski adapted by David Wood (Puffin Books, 1994)

The children's illustrated version of the play is on page 49 of the resource book.

Dinner with the Giants

Cast

NARRATOR	An Owl
GARTH	A Giant
HULK	A Giant
PAUNCH	A Giant
DIPPER	A Thief
SIMEON	A Sprite who can change shape

Plus non-speaking parts for **THREE ELVES**[1]

(***THE GIANTS** should try to make their speech distinctive in some way, such as using a high, low or squeaky voice. Someone who can mimic **THE GIANTS**' voices should play the part of **SIMEON**.*)[2]

ACT 1
SCENE 1

*(It is night time. **THREE GIANTS** are sitting round a fire in the mountains, noisily roasting chickens. **DIPPER** is hiding behind a rock watching them. **THE OWL** is perched far stage left.)*[3]

OWL: It is always a bad thing to be[4] near hungry mountain giants at night. How Dipper came to be in this situation was told to me by my friend, the Shape-Changer Sprite, Simeon.

A naughty witch had[5] cast a spell on the elves. This spell made them hiccup all the time. Simeon and the elves asked a well-known thief, Dipper, to go with them to see if he could[6] steal a spell to stop the hiccups. They had heard that such spells could be stolen[7] from a town full of witches that lay over the mountain. On their journey, they had stopped for the night at the foot of the mountain. Simeon had gone[8] off to find some water and the three elves had sent Dipper to investigate a light they could see further up the mountain. Dipper had climbed silently up until he came across the giants. He was hiding[9] behind a rock, watching the giants eat their supper. He was frightened that the giants might[10] catch him.

*(There is a sudden crash as one of **THE GIANTS**[11] throws a chicken onto the fire.)*

GARTH: Chicken, rabbits, frogs! Always blinkin' animals.[12]

HULK: Feels like I was a nipper since the last time I had eaten[13] humans. What we doin' 'ere anyways I don't know. And now the flippin' booze is running out.

*(**HULK** jogs **PAUNCH**'s elbow just as **PAUNCH** is about to take a gulp of his drink. **PAUNCH** chokes.)*[14]

PAUNCH: 'Ere you lot. Stop yer moaning. Do yer expect humans ought to wander by in case you fancy a nibble of their ears?[15] Was a time when you had been crying[16] for a tasty bit of chicken like this.

---

1. The characters in the play are listed and described at the beginning. The descriptions give us more information about the characters than can be gleaned from the dialogue and stage directions.

2. There is guidance on performing the roles.

3. The play is divided into five Acts. The words in italics set the scene for the Act.

4. 'To be' is an infinitive verb.

5. 'Had' is an auxiliary verb.

6. 'Could' is an auxiliary verb.

7. 'Be stolen' – passive voice of the verb 'to steal'.

8. 'Had gone' – past perfect tense of the verb 'to go'.

9. 'Was hiding' – past continuous tense of the verb 'to hide'.

10. 'Might' is an auxiliary verb.

11. The characters' names are written in capital letters. This informs the people playing the characters (actors) when they will be on stage and when they have action and/or dialogue to perform.

12. The actor should be aware of the punctuation here. The exclamation mark suggests indignation.

13. 'Had eaten' – past perfect tense of the verb 'to eat'.

14. The stage directions are in italics. This is a message for the director of the play, not the actor. The director tells the actor how this part should be acted.

15. Interrogative form of the verb 'to expect', requiring a 'yes'/'no' answer.

16. 'Had been crying – non-standard past tense of the verb 'to cry'. Standard English would be 'you cried' or 'you used to cry'.

(**PAUNCH** takes a huge bite from a whole chicken. **THE GIANTS** are grumbling[17] and mumbling while they eat.[18] **DIPPER** moves from rock to rock and then begins to creep towards **PAUNCH**.)

ACT 2
SCENE 1

OWL: As Simeon related to me, what the little thief did next was not as stupid as it may seem. Apparently, Dipper wanted to practise the stealing technique – and stealing from a giant's bag seemed like it would[19] be a good idea at the time.

(**DIPPER** puts his hand into **PAUNCH**'s huge bag. He pulls out an enormous watch. Immediately there is the ringing of a burglar alarm off stage. **DIPPER** drops the watch in amazement. **PAUNCH** turns, sees **DIPPER** and grabs him by the neck.)

PAUNCH: Cor lummy, Garth, good job me watch rings out if someone tries to nick it. 'Ere, look what I've collected![20]

GARTH: What the 'eck is it?

PAUNCH: Blowed if I know. (Addressing **DIPPER**) What are you?

DIPPER: Let me go.

HULK: A letmego? Letmegoes have been pinchin'[21] watches from our bags while we try and have a quiet bit o' supper then, aye?

GARTH: I bet it tastes nice.

HULK: (Picking up a skewer) Only one way we will find out.[22]

PAUNCH: Yuck. It's all dirty and smelly. We will be taking[23] off its skin and finding nothing but bones underneath.

GARTH: Might be a flock of 'em letmegoes about though. We could catch 'em and, with a bit of pastry, we shall have made[24] ourselves a tasty letmego pie. (Addressing **DIPPER**) Is there a flock of you a-flapping around here, eh?

DIPPER: Oh yes ... I mean, no, no, there's only me.

HULK: What d'yer mean?

DIPPER: What I said. Only please don't skin me and cook me. I'd taste awful. I'll do[25] anything you ask.

PAUNCH: He's frightened. Set him free.

GARTH: When he's told us what he means when he says there's a flock of letmegoes and then he says there's only him. He was a-pinchin' your watch, don't forget. If there's lots of 'em, we might all get robbed and killed while we sleep. We need[26] to start skinning him till he talks.

PAUNCH: Oh no you don't. I caught him. He's mine and I says set him free.[27]

17 'Are grumbling' – present continuous tense of the verb 'to grumble'.

18 'They eat' – simple present tense of the verb 'to eat'.

19 'Would' is an auxiliary verb.

20 'I've collected' – present perfect tense of the verb 'to collect'. 'I have' has been contracted.

21 'Have been pinchin'' – perfect and continuous aspects combined of the verb 'to pinch'.

22 'We will find out,' – future tense of the verb 'to find out'.

23 'We will be taking' – future continuous tense of the verb 'to take'.

24 'Shall have made' – future perfect tense of the verb 'to make'.

25 'I'll do' – future tense of the verb 'to do'. 'I will' has been contracted here.

26 'Need' is an auxiliary verb.

27 'Set him free' is an imperative.

HULK: You're addled, Paunch. You're an addle brain.

PAUNCH: And you're a dim wit.

HULK: Dim wit am I? Take <u>THAT!</u>[28]

(***HULK*** *pokes* ***PAUNCH*** *and* ***THE GIANTS*** *start fighting with a lot of noise.*)

<u>SCENE 2</u>

<u>(***THE GIANTS*** *continue to fight. During the fighting* ***DIPPER*** *gets knocked to the ground and is dazed.*)</u>[29]

<u>ACT 3</u>
<u>SCENE 1</u>

<u>OWL:</u> <u>The giants' fighting made so much noise that the elves crept up one by one to see what was happening. However, they hiccuped so loudly as they came near, the giants stopped fighting for enough time to tie each one up before they started fighting again. They forgot about Dipper who crept behind a rock again.</u>

<u>Simeon had returned to the elves' camp and found that everyone had disappeared, but he heard the noise the giants made. He changed himself into a bird and flew up to where the fight was going on. He saw three elves tied up and Dipper hiding behind a rock.</u>[30]

<u>SCENE 2</u>[31]

HULK: <u>Stop</u>[32] fighting! Let's get on with roasting these elves so's we can eat them later.

SIMEON: (*Mimicking* ***PAUNCH***'s voice) It'd take too long to roast 'em now.

GARTH: Stop arguing, Paunch. We've decided.

PAUNCH: I'm not arguing.

GARTH: Yes you are.

PAUNCH: Liar. I'm not.

(***THE THREE GIANTS*** *start fighting again.*)

<u>SCENE 3</u>

(***THE THREE GIANTS*** *finally stop fighting and lie on the floor, exhausted.*)

HULK: He's right though. It'd take all night to roast 'em.

PAUNCH: I never said.

GARTH: Did.

PAUNCH: Didn't.

28 The word is in capital letters to tell the actor how to say it. It is emphasised more than the others.

29 Scene 2 has no dialogue or narration. The whole scene consists of a noisy fight. The director would need to decide for himself how the actors should act the scene.

30 The whole of Scene 1 is told by the narrator. The actors should perform the actions.

31 In Scene 2 the dialogue begins again on stage.

32 'Stop' is an imperative.

HULK: Shut up. I say we chop 'em and boil 'em.

GARTH: That would cook 'em quick enough.

PAUNCH: All right, all right. Get the saucepan out and find yer choppers.

ACT 4
SCENE 1

(**_THE GIANTS_** _get out a huge saucepan and after much fussing about, find their axes and begin to sharpen them._)[33]

SCENE 2

SIMEON: (Mimicking **_HULK_**_'s voice_) It's no good boiling 'em. We ain't got no water and it's a long way to the river.

GARTH: Shut up Hulk, or we'll never get to eat them.

PAUNCH: Yeh Hulk, and you can go and get the water for moaning.

HULK: Don't you tell me to shut up and who's a-moaning? It weren't me.

PAUNCH: You liar Hulk; you big booby.

HULK: You're the liar Paunch and booby yerself.

(**_THE THREE GIANTS_** _start fighting again._)

SCENE 3

GARTH: Look, if we keep on fighting, the elves will rot before we get to eat 'em. I say we mash 'em and boil 'em later.

SIMEON: (Mimicking **_HULK_**_'s voice_) Who shall we mash first?

GARTH: Better mash the last one first.

HULK: Stop talking to yerself Garth. Anyways, which was the last one?

GARTH: That one with the loudest hiccups.

SIMEON: (Mimicking **_PAUNCH_**_'s voice._) Rubbish, the last one was the one with the quietest hiccups.

GARTH: I knows what I'm talking about, Paunch – the last one 'ad the loudest hiccups.

PAUNCH: Yes, he definitely had the loudest hiccups.

GARTH: So why did you say he had the quietest hiccups then?

PAUNCH: I never said; Hulk said it.

33 The words in brackets and italics are for the director to interpret for the actors.

HULK: No I never' you did.

GARTH: Hulk and I says you said it, so shut up.

PAUNCH: Who are you tellin' to shut up?

HULK: Stop arguing[34] – remember the saying among us mountain giants 'Never waste time near dawn'[35] – let's get cookin'.

SIMEON: (*Mimicking **PAUNCH**'s voice*) Dawn come and stone you!

ACT 5
SCENE 1

(*Sunlight appears over the mountain top and just as **THE THREE GIANTS** set to fighting again, they are turned to stone by the sunlight. **SIMEON**, as himself again, moves to centre stage, bringing **DIPPER** from behind the rock with him.*)

SCENE 2

DIPPER: Simeon! That was your voice causing them to argue until sunrise turned them into stone. You've saved us all from being part of a recipe. If it weren't for you we will have been cooking[36] in a pot.

SIMEON: Well, in case you are ever with giants again, Dipper, consider[37] this magic rune:

(***SIMEON** spreads his arms and lifts his head. There is complete silence.*)
Sunrise flutter the dark wings of nights
'Til the gloomy heavy shades have flown,
And icy dreams tangling fear and fights,
Are left behind and turned to stone.[38]

SCENE 3

(*The mountain is now lit by brilliant sunshine. **SIMEON** and **DIPPER** untie the still-hiccuping **ELVES**. There is much hugging and shaking of hands. The **ELVES** and **DIPPER** walk anxiously and curiously around the stone **GIANTS**. **SIMEON** looks on. Then, arm in arm, **THE ELVES**, **DIPPER** and **SIMEON** exit.*)

SCENE 4
(***OWL** stands still centre stage and spreads his wings.*)

OWL: The adventures of Simeon, Dipper and the Elves were just beginning. Will Dipper be able to steal the spell to stop the hiccuping? Will Simeon and the Elves be able to keep Dipper out of trouble until he does? Will Dipper learn his lesson and never steal again?[39]

(*The stage darkens; there is a clap of thunder and a flash of lightning. The light on stage dims until there is a blackout.*)[40]

34 Imperatives are used to instruct someone or something to do something.

35 This is a negative imperative.

36 'We will have been cooking' – future perfect continuous tense of the verb 'to cook', a non-standard use for the more usual 'We would have been cooking'.

37 Imperative to ask someone to think about a particular thing or possibility.

38 A play is a visual as well as an auditory experience. When writing a play, opportunities to write moments of dramatic intensity add to the visual and auditory dimensions.

39 Interrogative form of the verbs 'be', 'learn' and 'steal.

40 These directions involve backstage members of the drama group, such the person responsible for sound and lighting. It is worth remembering and emphasising the visual aspect of plays when writing them. The idea is to try to leave a strong visual impression with the audience.

Understanding the grammar

Grammar pointers

Verb tenses

Tense refers to time in relation to verbs. One test of whether or not a word is a verb is whether or not the tense can be changed. Verb tenses are: the past, the present and the future.

All verbs have a present and a past participle form. The present participle ends in 'ing' (for example, 'cooking'). Although it is called 'present' it is also used in the future continuous and the past continuous tense of a verb. The past participle often ends in 'ed' (for example, 'cooked') but can have other endings, for example 'en' (eaten).

Tenses can be simple or a main verb plus an auxiliary verb; the aspect can be be perfect (the action is complete) or continuous (the action is in progress).

The simple past and present uses one word which is a form of the main verb, for example:

simple past	*He ate it.*
simple present	*He eats it.*

The future usually involves 'will' or 'shall' (auxiliary verbs), for example:

> *He will eat it.*

The continuous aspect uses a tense of the verb 'to be':

past continuous	*He was eating it.*
present continuous	*He is eating it.*
future continuous	*He will be eating it.*

The perfect aspect of a verb uses a tense of the verb 'to have' and the past participle of the main verb:

past perfect	*He had eaten it.*
present perfect	*He has eaten it.*
future perfect	*He will have eaten it.*

The perfect and continuous aspects of a verb are often combined:

past perfect continuous	*He had been eating it.*
present perfect continuous	*He has been eating it.*
future perfect continuous	*He will have been eating it.*

Auxiliary verbs

An auxiliary verb is a verb used with the main verb to clarify the tense. Below is a list of auxiliary verbs:

> *do, can, could, may, might, must, am, is, are, has, have, had, ought to, shall, will, would, need to, dare, used, should.*

These auxiliary verbs change form depending on the tense used:

> auxiliary verb 'am' – *I am eating; I was eating I shall be eating.*

Verb forms

◆ Active

When using the active voice, the writer makes it clear who or what is performing the action of the verb.

> *The giant ate the elf.*

◆ Interrogative

The interrogative form can be questions that require a 'yes'/'no' answer:

> *Are you going to eat me?*

'Are' is an auxiliary verb; 'going' is the main verb. They can also be questions that begin with a 'wh' word (for example, 'why' and 'where').

> *What is a letmego?*

◆ Imperative

An imperative is a verb used in a sentence that gives orders or instructions.

> *Eat him.*

> *Fry him with chopped onion.*

Advice and warnings are given in the imperative form:

> *Don't be afraid.*

The imperative can also be used if the requirement is for someone to think about a particular thing or possibility or to compare something. Examples of these verbs are:

> *compare, contrast, look at, suppose, consider, imagine, picture, take.*

The children's version of these notes is on page 55 of the resource book.

Writing feature
Conventions of playscripting

How playscripts differ from stories

Explain to the children that playscripts tell a story but in a different way to those found in storybooks. Talk about the various differences:

◆ A playscript is to be performed for the entertainment of an audience.

◆ The audience will be entertained by seeing and hearing the performance. Therefore it is important for the play to be visually exciting as well as telling a good story.

◆ The work is organised into large sections called 'Acts'. Within these Acts the play is further divided into smaller sections called 'Scenes'. The writer of the play has to keep in mind the practicalities of changing scenes on a stage.

◆ The text is divided up in a special way. There are instructions that relate to stage directions, set production, costumes, lighting and sound as well as text to be read by the characters.

◆ In a story, every bit of text is meant to be read. In a play, only the actor's parts are read aloud.

◆ A story writer is able to write long, descriptive pieces to help the reader imagine the setting, characters and plot. A playwright is more limited. He has fewer descriptive tools to use and must develop the characters through the dialogue and by incorporating possibilities for the sets, costumes, lighting and sound to add atmosphere.

◆ The use of a narrator in a play must be carefully managed. A narrator can 'fill in' bits of the story that would not easily be managed in a playscript, but the narrator should be in character and should only give leads and small explanations of the action without taking over the entire story.

The layout of playscripts

Share various playscripts with the children. Discuss how they differ to stories and other texts. Point out that the font and typography is presented in different ways because it is meant for different people and purposes.

Discuss the following points:

ACT 1
SCENE 1

*(It is night time. **THREE GIANTS** are sitting round a fire in the mountains, noisily roasting chickens. **DIPPER** is hiding behind a rock watching them. **THE OWL** is perched far stage left.)*

OWL: It is always a bad thing to be near hungry mountain giants at night. How Dipper came to be in this situation was told to me by my friend, the Shape-Changer Sprite, Simeon.

◆ The play is divided up into larger sections called 'Acts' with shorter sections within them called 'Scenes'.

◆ The characters' names are written in capital letters in the stage directions and on the left-hand side of the page to indicate when a character is speaking and/or acting. The words to be spoken are set out in lines that are underneath each other.

◆ The scene setting is in italics. This is a message to the set designer, prop maker, costume maker, lighting manager and director. It tells us where the characters are and what the set should look like.

◆ The person playing the character reads aloud only the text that is not in brackets and does not read the character's name on the left-hand side.

◆ Sometimes some words in the dialogue are written using typography or punctuation to indicate how the words are to be spoken.

HULK: *Dim wit am I? Take THAT!*

The word 'that' is in capitals to tell the actor that he needs to emphasise this word.

There are helpful hints for children on writing a playscript on page 58 of the resource book.

Traditional West Indian stories

The West Indies has a strong African influence in its storytelling tradition. Most tales were brought from Africa to the Caribbean and often have an element of the supernatural or mysticism. Local folklore, history and superstition shape many of the storytelling traditions in the Caribbean and often familiar motifs are to be found in the tales.

Most West Indian characters earn their living by simple means, such as farming, working on the land and labouring. There is usually a wise person or an animal with human characteristics who helps the characters to overcome external problems or the darker side of their own selves.

Anansi appears in both African and West Indian tales. He is part-man, part-spider and is a trickster. However, he is also seen as wise and has certain endearing qualities, such as his laziness! Anansi often represents the virtuous conquering the wicked, although he can fall victim to his own lazy and cunning ways.

Music, dancing, carnivals, brightly-coloured garments and lyrical conversations are all key features of West Indian culture and are often used in various ways in the stories from these countries.

West Indian stories

Examples of West Indian stories

West Indian Folk Tales by Philip M Sherlock (OUP, 1994)

Duppy Talk: West Indian Tales of Mystery and Magic by Gerald Hausman (Irie Books, 1999)

Under the Storyteller's Spell edited by Charles Faustin (Viking Kestrel, 1989)

Anansi and The Golden Coconut by Sonja Dumas (Multimedia, 1990)

Cric Crac: West Indian Stories by Grace Hallworth (Heinemann, 1990)

Carnival by Grace Hallworth (Cambridge University Press, 1998)

The children's illustrated version of the story is on page 65 of the resource book.

Anansi and Hate-to-be-contradicted

There once was a man called Hate-to-be-contradicted[1], which is a strange name. He got the name because he was very bad-tempered and couldn't help disagreeing with people. One morning, a villager called on Hate-to-be-contradicted and they sat beneath his palm-tree as the sun beat down like fire.[2] As they sat talking, some palm-nuts fell to the ground.

"Hate-to-be-contradicted," said the villager, "your palm-nuts are ripe."

"No, they're not."

"Yes, look. Some have fallen. They're ready for picking."

"They are not ripe."

The villager was puzzled by Hate-to-be-contradicted's answer. Just then, some more palm-nuts fell to the ground.[3]

"See, more ripe palm-nuts have fallen," he exclaimed.[4]

Hate-to-be-contradicted grew hot and angry as he realised he was being contradicted.

"My palm-nuts will be ready when I say so and not before!" he shouted at the villager. "When palm-nuts are ripe, all the bunches on a branch open at the same time with a noise like a clap of thunder[5] and they tumble down on the head of anyone who disagrees with me. What do you think of that?"

"I think you are very stupid and very rude," said the villager, staring straight at Hate-to-be-contradicted.

"How dare you?" shouted Hate-to-be-contradicted, chasing the villager out of his courtyard with a stick in his hand. "You deserve a good beating for contradicting me!"

Over the next few months, Hate-to-be-contradicted had many disagreements and he became even more bad-tempered. He hit his neighbour with a broom because he would not agree that Hate-to-be-contradicted's dog had fewer fleas than his own. He threw his brother-in-law into a pond for refusing to agree that the moon was made of curdled cow's milk. Worst of all, he threw his cooking pot at some men for saying that the sun rose over their village before it rose over Hate-to-be-contradicted's village.[6]

The head of the village decided to ask Anansi, the spider, for advice. Anansi agreed to go and talk to Hate-to-be-contradicted. It was spring, the time of year when, once again, the palm-nuts were ripe.

"Good morning, Hate-to-be-contradicted,"[7] Anansi greeted him. "What a fine day it is."

Hate-to-be-contradicted was just about to disagree when he managed to stop himself. They sat beneath the shade of a palm-tree[8] and, as they were talking, some ripe palm-nuts fell to the ground. Hate-to-be-contradicted told Anansi his story about how to tell when palm-nuts were *really* ripe.

1 The name is symbolic, an example of figurative language, and tells the reader something of the character.

2 This is a complex sentence using the connective 'and'. A simile is used here to create a vivid image of the heat of the day ('as the sun beat down like fire').

3 'Some more' is a determiner for the noun 'palm-nuts'.

4 The pronoun 'he' is used here to avoid repetition of 'the villager'.

5 'A noise like a clap of thunder' is another example of figurative language, describing the ripening of the palm-nuts.

6 This passage contains several pronouns, used carefully to avoid confusion over who is being referred to. It also contains several complex sentences.

7 A comma precedes the character's name when he is being addressed directly.

8 'A' is a simple determiner for 'palm-tree'.

When he had finished, Anansi said, "I am sure that what you say is true. I have heard the thunderous sound when the bunches open at the same time, but you must come and see my sweet potato trees. They are so tall that I have to take my bow and arrow and shoot the sweet potatoes down one by one. What do you think of that, Hate-to-be-contradicted?"

Hate-to-be-contradicted began to argue but he decided to accept Anansi's invitation to see these sweet potato trees for himself. Anansi went home and told his children that Hate-to-be-contradicted was coming to visit. Sprinkling red palm-juice that looked like blood outside the door, he told his children, "When Hate-to-be-contradicted arrives, tell him that I am at the blacksmith's, having my arm mended."[9]

Hate-to-be-contradicted was furious that Anansi was not there to greet him but he tried to control his temper.

"Where is your mother?" he asked Anansi's children.

The children enjoyed telling tales. "When she was down at the stream today, she dropped her waterpot. While it was falling, she remembered the meal she had left cooking, so she came back to take the cooking-pot off the fire. Now she has gone back to catch the waterpot."[10]

Hate-to-be-contradicted was beside himself with rage but still, he managed to control himself. When Anansi came back, he invited Hate-to-be-contradicted to supper. The children served him a small fish on a huge pile of very hot peppers. Hate-to-be-contradicted took one mouthful and his mouth was an inferno.[11]

"Water," he gasped.

Anansi turned to his eldest child and asked her to bring some water for their guest.[12] A moment later, she reappeared without any water.[13]

"I am very sorry," the child explained, "but there is no water to spare. The water at the top of the pot belongs to father. The second layer is mother's and the bottom layer is our grandmother's. So, there is no water left for you."

Hate-to-be-contradicted exploded with fury.

"You lying offspring of a spider ..." he began, but Anansi stopped him with a sharp look.

"Mr Hate-to-be-contradicted," he said, "that isn't very polite. You are contradicting us. You have beaten other people for contradicting you so now we shall have to beat you!"

So, Anansi and his children beat Hate-to-be-contradicted until he broke into pieces. The pieces broke into smaller pieces and they were ground to powder which blew away on the wind to the far corners of the Earth[14]. That is why there is a little bit of Hate-to-be-contradicted in everyone, everywhere.

9 A complex sentence where the first subordinate clause begins with a verb.

10 We know that the pronoun 'she' refers to the children's mother because Hate-to-be-contradicted has just asked, "Where is your mother?"

11 A metaphor.

12 Although we do not know the child's name, it is not an important feature of the story. Sometimes less important characters can be nameless and this can avoid confusion for the reader.

13 This sentence begins with an adverbial phrase followed by a comma.

14 'Earth' here is a proper noun, referring to the world, rather than soil.

Understanding the grammar and punctuation

Understanding the grammar and punctuation enables children to control the language they use and therefore to write more interesting and powerful stories.

Grammar pointers

Nouns and pronouns

Discuss with the children that nouns denote people, objects, places and abstract entities. Remind them that nouns can usually be identified by the words 'the', 'a' or 'an' preceding them but that there may be additional words preceding the noun which describe or give further information about it.

Revise the different kinds of nouns – common nouns, proper nouns and collective nouns – as well as some of the exceptions to the rule for making nouns plural. Although generally, 's' or 'es' are used to pluralise nouns, there are some words, such as *child – children, man – men* and *person – people,* for example, which are pluralised differently.

Explain to the children that a noun phrase can be just one word or a group of words and may include a determiner:

> *a pond*
>
> *ripe palm-nuts*
>
> *He hit his neighbour **with a** broom.*

Children often overuse or misuse pronouns. Explain that a pronoun takes the place of a noun and that the verb must agree with the pronoun:

> *you were,* not *you was*

Encourage the children to reread their work frequently to ensure that it is clear to the reader who or what is being referred to when using pronouns. There should be a balance between nouns and pronouns so that neither dominates.

Punctuation pointers

Punctuating complex sentences

A complex sentence contains a main clause and one or more subordinate clauses. A subordinate clause generally starts with a subordinating conjunction (*as, whilst* or *although*) or relative pronoun (*who, which* and so on). The relative pronoun is sometimes merely suggested by the writer. The subordinate clause provides more information about the main clause, and usually does not make sense on its own.

Talk to the children about how useful complex sentences are because they enable us to compare ideas and pieces of information.

There are different ways to connect clauses. Subordinate clauses may begin with a subordinating conjunction such as *although, because* or *whenever.* For example:

> *He hit his neighbour with a broom because he would not agree that Hate-to-be-contradicted's dog had fewer fleas than his own.*

Sometimes the subordinate clause begins with a verb. For example:

> *Sprinkling red palm-juice that looked like blood outside the door, he told his children...*

When a sentence begins with a subordinate clause, a comma is placed directly after the opening clause. This makes it easier for the reader to follow the sense of the sentence. For example:

> *A moment later, she reappeared without any water.*

Explain to the children that they should place a comma before a name or term of address by which one character calls another when talking in direct speech. If the name occurs at the beginning of the sentence of speech, they should place the comma immediately after it. For example:

> *"Good morning, Hate-to-be-contradicted,"*
> *Anansi greeted him.*

The children's version of these notes is on page 68 of the resource book.

Writing feature
Using literal and figurative language

Literal language

Literal language is concerned with the use of words or phrases to convey an accurate and true meaning. It is a way of expressing an idea, event or feeling by describing, for example, exactly what was said/what something looked like/what happened.

> *Just then, some more palm-nuts fell to the ground.*

Literal language is used to avoid ambiguity or confusion and is commonly used in scientific, legal, medical and mathematical terminology, all of which necessitate clarity and precision.

Writers often use literal language in conjunction with figurative language for various effects. These may include providing the reader with a meaning that is commonly used in order to familiarise the reader with the characters and constructing a concrete rather than an abstract setting. The use of figurative language against this can have a striking and memorable effect on the reader.

Explain to the children that an object can be described literally by explaining its actual shape, colour, size and so on. Use examples of everyday objects, such as those found in the classroom, describing them literally and asking the children to guess what you are describing. They could then work in pairs or groups, making their own literal observations.

Figurative language

Figurative language is concerned with the use of words or phrases to convey a meaning other than their commonly used sense. In contrast to literal language, figurative language offers writers a wider choice of possibilities for conveying meaning in a more elaborate way. Figurative language employs a variety of methods of expressing ideas, such as similes, metaphors and idioms, all of which can paint a picture in words.

> *"When palm-nuts are ripe, all the bunches on a branch open at the same time with a noise like a clap of thunder."*

In this example, the simile *like a clap of thunder* is used to compare the noise of the ripening palm-nuts with something that the reader is likely to have experience of, ie thunder.

A metaphor is a form of figurative language that uses one thing to describe another. A metaphor differs from a simile in that, rather than comparing one thing to another, it exaggerates by stating that it is in fact something else:

> *his mouth was an inferno*

Idiomatic language is a conversational style of language in which some of the words and phrases have a meaning quite different from the literal; for example:

> *"That's really cool"* or *"He's a pain in the neck."*

Figurative language can also take the form of symbolism. The name, *Hate-to-be-contradicted* is used as a proper noun and is also the main characteristic of the character in the story.

There are helpful hints for children on writing a West Indian story on page 71 of the resource book.

Science fiction stories

A science fiction story explores consequences of improbable or impossible changes in the basic conditions of human or intelligent non-human life. The change is often a result of technological advances, but can also be a result of changes in biological or physical reality; for example, invasion by aliens, time travel or ecological dangers. Other familiar themes include encounters with aliens, space travel, the use of incredible gadgetry and life in the future. It is also possible, in science fiction writing, to imagine travel or experiences at a micro level; for example, journeys inside the human body where changes in size enable the characters to experience life as micro-organisms.

The human characters in science fiction stories are frequently surprisingly normal. This enables the reader to relate to their emotions and reactions in the face of extraordinary events.

Technical vocabulary and scientific wizardry are important features of science fiction writing. The author provides us with sensible names for incredible objects. Thus, most science fiction writing can be said to blend the fantastic with the familiar.

The mood of this genre can be sinister or light-hearted, its purpose to terrify, to inform or to amuse. However, most science fiction writing deals in some way with the problems encountered by people of the future despite, or perhaps owing to, the advanced science and technology of their society. Life is certainly not portrayed as being less problematical. These problems usually illustrate the consequences of a scientific or technological advance taken to extremes and so act as a warning or moral for the reader.

Writers of pure fantasy choose to create 'doors' from the real world into imaginary worlds that co-exist with our own. These other worlds frequently contain magical creatures and incredible settings. When characters pass from the real world into a fantasy world, they often acquire new understanding and abilities. Sometimes these are needed to help the inhabitants of the fantasy world to solve a problem and through this the writer gives us more insight into aspects of everyday life.

Science fiction stories

Examples of science fiction stories

My Teacher is an Alien by Bruce Coville (Collins, 2000)

Midnight Blue by Pauline Fisk (Lion, 2001)

Memoirs of a Dangerous Alien by Maggie Prince (Orion, 1996)

Meteorite Spoon by Philip Ridley (Puffin, 2000)

(For advanced readers)

Earthdark by M. Hughes, retold by John Escott (Penguin, 1995)

The children's illustrated version of the story is on page 78 of the resource book.

A World of Difference

At dusk the silver orbs gathered and hung in the <u>sky</u>,[1] like a still, silent <u>flock</u>[2] of birds. People would remark on their shining beauty as the clouds, streaked with the colours of sunset, were reflected in their glittering shapes.

When they had first appeared everyone had panicked. Newspapers carried headlines like '<u>Invasion of Silver Spheres</u>' and '<u>Decorations or Devastation?</u>'[3] Countries tried everything possible to catch or destroy them. The silver orbs, the size of tennis balls, simply zipped out of the way and carried on floating. The orbs never did any harm, but just seemed to spiral about wherever there were people. Bit by bit interest faded. <u>They were as normal as the clouds themselves and just as elusive.</u>

<u>It was definitely odd, therefore, to see one bumping along the grass</u>[4] heading for the woods. <u>Sarah</u>[5] and <u>Jack</u>[5] had been arguing as usual. This time they had argued <u>about: meteorites, black holes and eternity</u>.[6] Sarah was small, with a freckled, determined face and Jack was tall, dark and a bit moody. The strange sight of <u>the silver orb</u>[7] rolling past them caused a moment's truce.

"I've never seen one do that before," Jack murmured.

"We'd better follow it – see what happens," Sarah said eagerly, moving forwards.

Jack caught hold of her sleeve. "Don't be silly, Sarah. It's going into the woods; it could be dangerous."

Sarah shrugged him off. "No one said you had to come if you're too scared," she snarled.

"I can't let you go on your own, something might happen to you." <u>Jack was trying to be reasonable.</u>[8]

"Well, you'd better come then," Sarah said impatiently and ran off after the orb.

<u>"You're impossible, Sarah – Sarah – wait!" Jack shouted, but she'd gone. Jack had no choice but to follow her.</u>[9]

The children pursued the orb as it bounced and rolled over the roots of trees, spinning deeper into the woods. There was no hope of catching it, but the orb seemed to know exactly where it was going. When it stopped, Jack and Sarah crept behind a tree, wondering what it was going to do next. As they watched, a light started to glow in front of them. It brightened and hardened into a metal cylinder as high as the trees. A gap in its side began to widen. The small silver orb rolled towards it.

"Come on, Jack. It's going in. Let's follow it," Sarah whispered.

"Are you mad?" Jack screeched.

"Shush, there's no time to argue now. Coming or not? I'm going in."

1   A common noun.

2   A collective noun.

3   Signs, headlines and adverts are often contracted sentences.

4   Moving from the general to the specific is a useful story-writing technique.

5   Proper nouns. People's names always begin with a capital letter.

6   Using a colon in a list.

7   A simple noun phrase incorporating an adjective.

8   Written speech is interactive and involves taking turns. A character's 'turn' can be indicated in other ways than by using 'said' or alternatives for 'said'. In this case, the speaker's mood is used.

9   Characterisation has been shown through the use of different speech patterns and the use of verbs. Sarah has been described using words such as 'eagerly', 'shrugged' and 'snarled', showing her to be impatient and headstrong. Jack has been shown to be more cautious.

Sarah darted forward again. Jack groaned, fear clutching at his stomach as he went after her. The little orb bounced through the doorway in the side of the huge metal cylinder. Sarah, followed closely by Jack, slipped in behind it: a heavy door silently slid shut behind them.[10]

"Now look what's happened," Jack growled. "We're trapped."

The children were standing in a small, dim chamber. Low, ultraviolet light oscillated through tubes that stretched along the sheer chrome walls.[11]

"Jack," Sarah clutched his arm, "we're floating off the ground!"

Jack looked down. His feet were hovering about five centimetres from the floor.

"It must be a slightly different gravitational pull in here," Jack said, "and we're not wearing g-suits."

Sarah wasn't too sure what g-suits were (though she wasn't going to admit that to Jack).[12]

"So what? We can breathe. Where would we get these suits from anyway? Marks and Spencer?" Sarah laughed and slapped her hand against the metallic wall. The sound echoed through the chamber so loudly that Sarah stopped suddenly. In the cold silence that followed, a low beeping sound began. This was followed by a mechanised voice saying, "Echo pulse activated... Echo pulse activated..."

An elderly figure appeared, coming towards them in the gloom. His white hair was parted in the middle of his rather large head. He was wearing a long cloak, but as he approached there didn't seem to be any sign of his legs moving underneath it. He pulled out a signal display unit and, after he had pushed a few buttons, the beeping and the mechanised voice fell silent. He turned and folded his arms.[13]

"Oh dear. Visitors," he sighed. He looked at the silver orb that was gently quivering by now.

"You've got a malfunction. Off you go to maintenance," said the old man.

The orb bumped off into the darkness. Turning to the children he said, "I expect you'll want explanations and everything now."

Sarah and Jack looked at each other. Before Sarah could say anything rude, Jack, pressing his back against the door, said hurriedly, "Well, it's a bit of a shock, of course, but if you don't mind we'll just go home now. We won't say anything to anyone."

"Of course you will – but no one will believe you.[14] Don't worry, you're quite safe," smiled the man. "My name's Zenith by the way and you two are from the twenty-first century. You have found your way into the Planet Earth Humanoid Laboratory. We have other humanoid observatories in different galaxies[15] of course. The silver orbs that seem to puzzle all you humans so much, are a bit like your camcorders, but we call them scopes. Through them, we watch everything you do. We're here to watch all the parallel Earths."[16]

"Parallel Earths?" Sarah muttered, looking a bit stunned.

---

10 Using a colon to separate clauses in a sentence.

11 Use of technical or scientific language is important in a science fiction story.

12 Punctuation can be used to indicate intonation. In this case, brackets are used to show that Sarah's next words are defensive.

13 In this passage, nouns, pronouns and verbs agree. The verb tense used is the same throughout and the third person singular is used. By not using any other pronouns, the meaning is kept clear.

14 Using a dash to replace other types of punctuation, in this case a comma.

15 A noun phrase using the preposition 'in'.

16 In science fiction stories, other worlds do not have to be on other planets.

"Yes," said Zenith. "There are many civilisations all taking place at the same time on this planet. They are all at different stages of technological development. Yours is still in a right mess. You haven't decided yet what to become expert at and you're all fighting each other. <u>One day you'll learn to discuss things reasonably.</u>[17] However, it's still a <u>very interesting piece of research for us."</u>[18]

"What are you talking about?" Sarah snapped, rather offended at being associated with 'a right mess'.

"Let me show you round; you might understand then," Zenith said.

They followed him down a long, twisting corridor. As they went, they passed doors with signs on, like 'Robotic Earth'.

"They've become experts at advanced robotics in that parallel," explained Zenith.

They passed other doors, <u>such as; 'Space Travel Earth', 'Virtual Reality Earth' and 'Microbiology Earth'</u>[19] with Zenith explaining as they went. Eventually they came to a door with a large red cross on it. A sign on the door said 'Clone Earth'. <u>Zenith sighed and shook his head.</u>[20] "This is very sad," he said. "This Earth was doing well, but they took it too far. Oh yes, they got rid of diseases and wars, but there's no longer any development. They all look the same; they all agree. What they need is to start having their own opinions again; think differently from each other. Even their books say the same thing. There is only one television programme and one film that they watch over and over again. <u>I'm afraid we're going to have to zap it."</u>[21]

"<u>*Zap it?*</u>"[22] said Jack and Sarah together. "You can't do that!"

"You can go in and see for yourselves if you like. You never know, you might come up with something that will save them," Zenith said. "Don't worry, they'll only think you're ghosts if they see you at all. When you want to come out, simply say so to one of the scopes that we've put in there."

Sarah could sense that Jack would find some reason why they shouldn't go, so she said quickly, "Hurry up and let us in."

"Now look here, Sarah," Jack began, but Zenith had opened the door and with a little push from him, the children found themselves in Clone Earth. They had landed in a classroom. All the children looked exactly the same. Even the teacher looked just like an older version of the children. Everyone was working in total silence. The children were drawing pictures, but every picture was a <u>carbon copy</u>[23] of everyone else's. <u>They were pictures of a garden; all had exactly eleven flowers and two trees.</u>[24] No one seemed to notice Jack and Sarah. Jack sat down on an empty chair and put his head in his hands. He looked very fed up.

"Jack, let's go back to Zenith. We can't let him destroy this Clone Earth or whatever it's <u>called – there's</u>[25] got to be a way to save it." Sarah said.

Jack nodded and went up close to a silver scope that was floating by one of the children. <u>He</u>[26] mumbled, "We'd like to come back now." Instantly, they were in front of Zenith again.

"Well?" the old man said.

17 This is a clue to one of the 'morals' of the story. Science fiction stories often carry a moral about the conditions on Earth.

18 Although Zenith is an alien, he appears to be fairly human. However, difference is established, not only by some small details of appearance, but also by his objective attitude to life on Earth.

19 Using a semicolon for a list.

20 Who is speaking can be indicated by gesture.

21 Another indicator of Zenith's very objective attitude to life on Earth.

22 Italics can indicate the intonation of a character's speech.

23 A noun phrase that uses another noun, 'carbon', as an adjective.

24 Using a semicolon to separate clauses in a sentence.

25 Punctuation, this time a dash, can indicate a pause.

26 The pronoun 'he' is clearly referring to Jack as it follows Jack's actions.

Sarah looked thoughtful. "Now look here, Zenith,"[27] she began. Jack groaned. "Shut up, Jack. Zenith, we don't know what to do yet, but we want to come back and visit Clone Earth until we find a solution."

Zenith thought for a moment. "Well, it's highly irregular," he mused, "but I don't like zapping Earths. I'll give you until ... let's see.[28] It's your summer holidays[29] now, isn't it?" Jack and Sarah nodded. "I'll give you until the end of your autumn half term. That's the best I can do. However, I'll know by looking at the scopes if you tell anyone about all this. Our laboratory will simply find another materialisation spot and I'm afraid you won't have the opportunity to help Clone Earth. I'm sure that won't happen, so, when you want to come back again, just speak to a scope and the laboratory will wait here in the woods for you."

During the weeks that followed, Jack and Sarah visited Clone Earth many times. They went to all its different countries at different times of day and night. Every time they went, Jack and Sarah argued about where to go and what to do. As time went on and they still had no idea how to save Clone Earth, their arguments got worse and worse. They were often seen by people. Many of them didn't believe their eyes and thought they[30] were dreaming. Others thought they were ghosts and would scream and run away. Their one newspaper carried headlines like 'Ghosts Spotted All Over' and 'Dreaming Scientists Study New Phenomena'.[31] However, some would stay and listen to them and a few even joined in with their arguments. The end of autumn half term came, but Jack and Sarah had not come up with any solution. Although they pleaded in front of the silver scopes[32] that floated in their homes, Planet Earth Humanoid Laboratory no longer materialised in the woods. It seemed they had failed Clone Earth.

It was in this mood of despondency that Sarah and Jack were putting up Christmas decorations a month or so later.

"I can't believe Zenith would have destroyed Clone Earth. He couldn't," Jack sighed.

Sarah angrily marched up to a scope that was hovering in her sitting room. "If you're watching, Zenith, I know human life doesn't mean anything to you, does it? We're all just like animals in a zoo, aren't we?" she shouted.

"Oh stop it, Sarah!" Jack snapped. Sarah was just about to turn on Jack for yet another argument, when she noticed a face appearing in the shining surface of the scope. It was Zenith!

"Ah, Sarah," Zenith said. "Glad to see you're still your argumentative self. I just thought I'd give you an update on Clone Earth."

Jack tried to push Sarah out of the way, but he had to make do with looking over her shoulder.

"Well, there hasn't been a lot of change, I'm afraid," Zenith sighed. The brief fluttering of hope that the children had felt, died. "However, there does seem to be a bit of an interesting problem. It began with the people of Clone Earth discussing whether or not ghosts existed. This developed into heated debates about all sorts of things and now I'm afraid there are outbursts of positive rows going on there. We've decided to give them a few millenniums[33] to see what happens, though with all this quarrelling..."

But Sarah and Jack were jumping around, hugging each other,[34] shouting, "We made them argue! We saved them! Merry Christmas Clone Earth," and they didn't hear another word he said.

27 Sarah usually speaks imperatively to show her strong personality.

28 Punctuation, in this case an ellipsis, can indicate a pause while a character thinks.

29 A noun phrase using a possessive determiner.

30 Using pronouns needs special care to avoid confusion. It is just possible that the 'they' used here means Sarah and Jack.

31 Using contractions can sometimes create ambiguity. The ghosts could be covered in spots and the scientists could be dreaming or scientists who study dreaming.

32 This reinforces the difference between the alien Zenith and us. He thinks of time in a different way. It seems that a millennium is a short time to him.

33 Although Jack and Sarah have not adopted one moral of the story, that of talking things through reasonably, it is clear that their friendship can overcome their differences of opinion.

Understanding the grammar and punctuation

Grammar pointers

Nouns

Nouns are used to identify a person, place or thing. Nouns can be singular or plural. Common nouns are general names common to all things, such as:

sky, sunset, orb

Proper nouns refer to a particular person, place or ⋯ begin with

⋯ ings, it is

⋯ ke its
noun
⋯ er a
⋯ y another
⋯ specific

⋯ mation
⋯ y often
⋯ niner. For

Pronouns stand in for nouns to avoid repetition and to show how the subject and object of a clause are related. For example:

Sarah saw the sphere and followed it.

To avoid confusion when two or more things are mentioned, the noun or noun phrase must be repeated. For example:

The silver sphere glided slowly along the forest floor. The sphere shone in the moonlight. (Or the reader could think the forest floor shone in the moonlight.)

There are many types of pronoun. Pronouns include: I, you, he, she, it, mine, yours, theirs, hers, myself, themselves, himself, this, that, these, those, anybody, somebody, something, nothing, no one, each other, one another, who, whom, which, that, whose, what, which.

Punctuation pointers

The use of punctuation to replace intonation, pauses or gestures

Punctuation can be used to indicate pauses clearly, but its use for gesture and intonation requires some inference from the reader. For example:

A semicolon separates two main clauses in a sentence and takes the place of a comma.

Sarah liked the Clone Earth people; they didn't argue with her.

Ellipses can be used to replace words and a sense of drama is created.

I'll give you until ... let's see.

Dashes can replace any other form of punctuation and create a dramatic pause.

"Of course you will – but no one will believe you."

Brackets can be used to indicate the character's feelings/reactions.

Sarah wasn't too sure what g-suits were (though she wasn't going to admit that to Jack).

Ambiguities

Sentences are sometimes contracted, or shortened, to give impact. This often happens in newspaper headlines and advertisements. Ambiguities arise when more than one meaning can be understood from what is written:

'Ghosts Spotted All Over'.

This could mean that the ghosts are covered in spots or that people have seen ghosts all over the place.

> The children's version of these notes is on page 83 of the resource book.

Writing feature
Story endings

The ending of a story is of paramount importance as, to a certain extent, it determines the reader's lasting impression of a book. Endings have certain functions in a short story: they solve whatever problems have arisen in the story in order to conclude it and they also usually indicate whether or not the characters have changed or learned anything from the experiences they underwent during the story.

When the children are planning their story, they need, therefore, to keep the events in the story to a minimum. The events have to lead to a conclusion – a solving of a problem. Too many events will lead to confusion and a rambling, incoherent structure.

There is a wide variety of different story endings. Fairytales usually have the 'and they all lived happily ever after' sort of ending. Adventure stories are usually concerned with a happy future and the triumph of the hero or heroine. Detective stories reveal the criminal, which is often a surprise to the reader. Some stories have sad or bittersweet endings.

To help the children appreciate the importance of story endings, try looking at the endings of nursery rhymes and ask them to tell a different story leading up to the ending. Reading unfamiliar story endings to the children and asking them to infer the rest of the story can extend this activity.

Interesting story endings can be created by subverting the overall 'happiness ever after' scenario. Choose some well known fairytales and see if the children can suggest alternative endings – ones that show not all will be perfect after all!

Discussing television programmes and films is also a useful way of showing how effective endings can be. Many science fiction films end in some sort of world disaster, but the characters find solutions in personal relationships.

Some effective story endings use ellipses, dashes, exclamation marks and brackets to show that the story may have a sequel of some sort or that a twist or surprise has occurred.

In the story 'A World of Difference', the events are structured so that there is a change in the normal world of Sarah and Jack. This change is the peculiar behaviour of one of the spheres. The plot moves on to the problem of Clone Earth. The events move simply between the change and the problem, with each event being expanded upon within a few paragraphs, in a step-by-step construction.

The solving of the problem is delayed. Through past experiences with stories, the reader will expect a solution to the story's problem. The story could have concluded at the line 'It seemed they had failed Clone Earth' but this would leave the reader feeling vaguely dissatisfied. By delaying the solution, it is possible that their expectations are slightly subverted.

The solution is not explicitly spelled out by Zenith. As an alien he is unaware that a millennium for humans is a very long time.

The ending makes it clear that Sarah and Jack need not worry too much about the fact that they argue a lot – their experiences in Clone Earth show that differences of opinion create development.

> There are helpful hints for children on writing a science fiction story on page 86 of the resource book.

Irish legends

Irish legends have been passed from one generation to the next, often by word of mouth, for over 2000 years. This unit contains two scaffolds: one for writing different versions of the legend of King Larry, and one for writing a legend about Finn, son of Cumhall.

There are many legends about Finn and the Fianna, the army of soldiers that he led. (Indeed, accounts of epic battles and acts of heroism against a dangerous foe are common features of these ancient stories.) In summer, the Fianna spent their time hunting and fishing, and for the rest of the year they served the High King, whose home was at Tara.

Many Irish legends are about doomed love affairs or cruel sorcery, and are almost unbearably sad. *Deirdre of the Sorrows* is one example. At Deirdre's birth, it is prophesied that her beauty will result in the deaths of many men, and this proves to be the case. In *The Children of Lir* and *The Story of Oisin and Niamh*, relief is finally brought to the suffering characters by holy men of the Church.

As well as being accomplished fighters, the Fianna had to be able to recite twelve books of poetry! There are frequent references to poetry and music, particularly the music of the harp and the pipes, in Irish legends. In the second scaffold in this unit, Finn's supernatural enemy lulls all mortals to sleep with his magical music.

In addition to great warriors, soldiers and kings, Irish legends contain sea monsters, giants, dragons, druids (pagan priests who were wise and had magical powers) and fairies. The fairies (the Sidhe) lived underground in the Land of Youth (Tir Na n'Og), but at Hallowe'en (Samhain) and on May Day a passage appeared between their world and the human world, and the fairies visited mortals. Other supernatural figures of Irish legend are the leprechauns. They were little people who usually had a hidden pot of gold.

The landscape of these Celtic legends is that of Ancient Ireland: windswept beaches, islands with rocky shores, vast forests, fast-flowing rivers, green meadows, blackberry-filled hedgerows and fields of ragwort. The hazel tree was a symbol of love, and the rowan tree was considered to have magical properties. Many legends also refer to the creatures of the countryside: the deer, salmon, wild boar and eagle.

In common with all Irish legends, the story in this unit illustrates a moral principle.

Irish legends

Examples of Irish legends

Celtic Fairy Tales retold by Philip Wilson (Mustard, 1999)

Etain and Midir illustrated by Heather McKay (Owl Records Ltd, 1997)

Finn and the Wicked Fairy of Tara retold by Reg Keating (Owl Records Ltd, 1997)

Great Irish Legends for Children retold by Yvonne Carroll (Quadrillion Publishing Ltd, 1999)

Irish Fairy Tales and Legends retold by Una Leavy (Orchard Books, 1996)

Irish Legends for Children retold by Yvonne Carroll (Zigzag Publishing Ltd, 1994)

Irish Myths and Legends retold by Ita Daly (OUP, 2001)

The Names Upon the Harp retold by Marie Heaney (Faber and Faber Ltd, 2000)

(For advanced readers)

Irish Fairy Tales illustrated by Arthur Rackham (Wordsworth, 1995)

The Tain by Liam Mac Uistin (The O'Brien Press Ltd, 1989)

The children's illustrated version of the story is on page 93 of the resource book.

How Finn became leader of the Fianna

As <u>Finn MacCumhall</u>[1] approached the palace of the <u>High King</u>[2], he noticed that the road snaking ahead of him shimmered with a magical silver light. It was <u>Hallowe'en</u>[3], and Finn was on his way to tell the king of Ireland that he wanted to serve him as a member of <u>the Fianna, the special band of warriors that Finn's father had once led.</u>[4]

Finn shivered. Was it because the air was bitterly cold, or was it because this was the night when the doorway opened between the world of the fairies and the world of mortals, and strange events occurred? Kneeling down beside his hound, <u>Bran</u>[5], Finn buried his face in the dog's warm coat.

"We haven't far to go now, Bran," he murmured. "Look, you can see the lights blazing in the feasting hall."

And, indeed, at that very moment, a magnificent banquet was taking place in the great hall of Tara. <u>Harpists</u>[6] played as the king and his soldiers feasted on roast meats. Jugs of mead and plates piled high with delicious food were passed from man to man. The king had ordered that old grudges should be forgotten, and this company of fierce fighters sat as meekly as lambs.

Boom! Boom! Boom! Who was that knocking on the great oak door?

"Enter!" commanded the king.

Everyone in the hall turned towards the newcomer. He was tall and his back seemed broad enough to carry three men of normal stature. But the most striking thing about the stranger was <u>his hair. It fell to his shoulders and was the colour of a pool of golden sunlight in a forest clearing</u>[7]. At the man's side was an enormous hound.

"My name is Finn MacCumhall," said the young man, kneeling before the king, "and I have come to offer you my service."

Now everyone in the hall turned to look at Goll MacMorna, for it was he who had killed Finn's father. The room was so quiet that you could hear the grass growing in the fields outside the city walls.

"You are welcome," replied the king. "Your father was a great <u>warrior –</u>[8] and he was also one of my closest friends. But I warn you not to seek to avenge his death here tonight. There will be peace among men at this feast."

"I will fight no one here, oh king, only your enemies," promised Finn.

"Then be seated beside my son, Art."

After the meal was over, the men listened to poetry about the great heroes of the past. Finally the king stood up. The light in his eyes had gone out, and all of a sudden he seemed like an old man.

"Friends, for the last nine years on the night of Hallowe'en, Tara has been attacked by a creature from the fairy world, a dragon so terrible that, until now, no soldier has been able to save my palace from it. Unless one of you

1. There are many legends about Finn MacCumhall (anglicised as Finn MacCool). After his father's death, his mother entrusted him to the care of two women warriors, who taught him fighting skills. He then went to live with a poet, in order to learn to recite poetry. (This was an entry requirement for the Fianna, the band of soldiers that Finn's father had once led.) The poet succeeded in catching the Salmon of Knowledge. It was said that whoever ate this fish would know everything that there was to know in the world. While he was cooking the salmon for the poet, Finn mistakenly tasted it: he popped a blister on the side of the fish with his thumb, and then put his thumb in his mouth to soothe it. From then on, Finn only had to suck his thumb in order to find the solution to any problem!

2. The palace of the High King of Ireland was at Tara.

3. At Hallowe'en (Samhain) a passageway was said to open between the mortal world and the world of the fairies, and strange, magical happenings occurred.

4. Cumhall, Finn's father, was a brave, accomplished leader of the Fianna. He was killed by Goll MacMorna at the battle of Castleknock.

5. Bran is mentioned in many of the legends about Finn. Bran and another hound discover the beautiful faun that turns into a maiden, who becomes Finn's wife.

6. There are references to the music of the harp and the pipes in many Irish legends.

7. In Irish Gaelic, the name Finn means 'white' or 'fair'.

8. The dash is used here rather than a comma for dramatic effect.

is willing to stand up to the evil beast, I know that tomorrow morning this magnificent hall will be nothing <u>but ...</u>[9] a heap of smouldering ashes. Who amongst you will help me?"

For a moment there was silence. Then Finn rose to his feet and said bravely, "It would be an honour for me to be your champion, oh king. I will protect Tara from this monster."

<u>After he had taken up his sword and shield,</u>[10] he strode out of the great hall, followed by Bran.

"That's the last we'll see of him," whispered Goll MacMorna to his neighbour.

Crunch! Crunch! Crunch! The sound of Finn's footsteps echoed through the darkness as he made his way towards the lonely city walls. <u>Although he could feel his heart pounding inside his chest,</u>[11] Finn was glad that the king had given him the chance to prove himself. <u>It seemed that his whole life had been a sort of preparation for this night, for this fight.</u>[12]

Out of the inky blackness came a voice that startled Finn. He peered into the gloom and was just able to make out a pair of gleaming eyes.

"Finn, before your father died, he saved my life at the battle of Castleknock. <u>Now I want to help you. Take this spear</u>.[13] It is magic, and will give you the power to stay awake when the dragon plays its enchanted music of sleep. When Bran barks, place the spear against your forehead. I must go, for I fear the dragon above all things."

Before Finn could thank the man, he had vanished, swallowed up in the murk of the night. Finn scarcely had time to examine the mysterious carvings on the spear before Bran began to bark. (<u>You see, a dog can hear sounds long before a man, and Bran sensed that the unearthly music floating towards Tara over the tree tops was dangerous and deadly.</u>)[14]

Bran's barking made Finn realise that he was becoming drowsy, so he quickly did as the stranger had advised him and placed the cold blade of the weapon against his brow. The metal roused him, bringing him to his senses! He felt as though he had just walked through the waterfall in the woods <u>where he had lived as a boy</u>[15]. What a narrow escape! He had nearly fallen under the spell of the dragon's music!

<u>Finn gazed in horrified wonder at the immense creature winging its way towards him.</u>[16] Its cruel, bulging eyes were like red-hot coals. Its once iridescent scales were charred and dull. It carried with it the stench of death. The dragon's wings beat through the air powerfully, fanning the flames of his fiery breath. Each gasp of air taken by Finn scorched his chest. His shield was melting, but the magic spear remained cool. He pressed the blade onto his forehead.

The dragon launched a vast missile of fire on Tara. In a flash, Finn whipped off his cloak, a cloak that had been given to him by his father, and used it to smother the sheet of flame. Fearlessly he leapt onto the dragon's back. The demonic creature screeched in fury and writhed in the air, struggling to shake Finn off. But Finn was too strong for him. He plunged his magic spear into the dragon's shoulder. The creature's death-cry was enough to chill the blood of all honest people from Tara to Dublin. With one blow of his sword, Finn smote the dragon's head from its body. Bran barked triumphantly!

9 An ellipsis is used to show the manner in which the character speaks – the High King hesitates before uttering the words that are so abhorrent to him: that Tara will be nothing but ashes.

10 A comma follows the subordinate clause that begins this complex sentence. The subordinate clause begins with the conjunction 'after'.

11 A comma again separates the subordinate clause from the main clause that follows it.

12 Many Irish legends contain a fierce struggle or a battle between the forces of good and evil.

13 The short sentences help to create suspense and tension, as well as being characteristic of speech. (Placing long sentences consecutively establishes a calm, restful mood.)

14 This direct comment to the reader draws him/her into the story.

15 The women warriors raised Finn in Slieve Bloom.

16 Fearsome monsters like this dragon from the fairy world Tir Na n'Og (the Land of Youth) are present in several Irish legends.

What a commotion there was when Finn presented the High King with the head of the dragon! The Fianna cheered and banged their fists on the table in delight; the harpists played their most uplifting melodies; and the poets put their heads together to compose a poem in honour of Finn.

"Finn, you have saved Tara from the flames of this hideous creature. I owe you a tremendous debt. How can I repay you?" asked the High King.

"By making me leader of the Fianna, as my father would have wished," replied Finn.

"Then so be it. What say you, Goll MacMorna[17]?" MacMorna considered his reply to the king's enquiry carefully.

"I pledge my loyalty to you, Sire, and to the new leader of the Fianna, Finn MacCumhall!" he cried.

That is the legend of how Finn came to lead the Fianna. He proved to be a wise, brave leader; indeed the most famous leader that the Fianna ever had![18]

17 At that time, Goll MacMorna was leader of the Fianna, but he was unpopular.

18 This Irish legend has a happy ending. The moral lesson of the story is that bravery and virtue will be rewarded. Men should remain loyal to their king, and should repay one another for virtuous deeds.

Understanding the grammar and punctuation

Understanding the grammar and punctuation enables children to control the language they use and therefore to write more interesting and powerful stories.

Grammar pointers

Types of sentences

A **simple** sentence contains **one clause**. This means that it has one idea or action and one verb.

> *The dragon's wings beat through the air powerfully.*

A **compound** sentence has **two or more clauses** often joined by *or*, *and*, *but*, or *so*.

> *The dragon was very big, but it did not frighten Finn.*

A **complex** sentence has **a main clause**, which could make sense on its own, and **one or more subordinate clauses**, which depend on the main clause for their meaning.

> *The dragon's wings beat through the air powerfully, fanning the flames of his fiery breath.*

The first part of the sentence is the main clause. It makes sense on its own.

Conjunctions

A subordinate clause usually begins with a **conjunction**.

Common subordinating conjunctions are: *after, although, as, as soon as, because, before, in case, in order to, now, since, so, until, when, whenever, where, wherever, while.*

> *After he had taken up his sword and shield, he strode out of the great hall, followed by Bran.*

Punctuation pointers

Punctuating complex sentences

When you begin a sentence with a subordinate clause, you put a comma after the subordinate clause. This makes it easier for the reader to follow the sense of the sentence.

> *Although he could feel his heart pounding inside his chest, Finn was glad that the king had given him the chance to prove himself.*

Punctuating direct speech

There are three main patterns of speech:

Type 1
The speech comes first in the sentence.

> *"That's the last we'll see of him," whispered Goll.*

Notice that the spoken words are enclosed in speech marks. (These are also known as inverted commas.) A comma is placed directly after the speech, and before the closing speech mark.

Type 2
The speech comes at the end of the sentence.

> *Then Finn rose to his feet and said bravely, "It would be an honour for me to be your champion, oh king. I will protect Tara from this monster."*

The speech is introduced by a comma, which is placed before the opening speech mark. The first spoken word begins with a capital letter as it is the first word in the sentence of speech.

Type 3
The speech is split; it is placed at the beginning and end of the main sentence.

> *"My name is Finn MacCumhall," said the young man, kneeling before the king, "and I have come to offer you my service."*

A comma is placed before the speech mark which follows the first part of the speech. Another comma stands in front of the second set of speech marks. Notice that the first word of the second part of the speech does not begin with a capital. This is because it is the second part of the sentence of speech.

Writing dialogue
In stories, you start a new paragraph every time there is a new speaker.

> *"You can tell your secret to the willow tree, Fergus," said his mother.*

> *"But King Larry made me promise not to speak of it to any living creature," he replied sadly.*

> *"A tree is a living thing, but it is not a living creature," Mrs O'Hanlon assured him.*

The children's version of these notes is on page 96 of the resource book.

Writing feature
Using direct speech

Why we use direct speech in stories

Explain to the children that speech serves lots of purposes, or fulfils several functions, in their stories.

✦ Starting a story with interesting direct speech (words spoken by a character) immediately gains the reader's interest. For example:

> *"I want to tell you about something very strange that happened to me when I was a boy," said the old man mysteriously, drawing his chair closer to the fire.*

✦ Speech can also be used to create an enthralling ending for the story.

> *James knew then that he'd made a big mistake. "You'll never see me again," she said bitterly. And he never did.*

✦ Speech gives variety to a narrative.

✦ The words spoken by a character give the reader insight into what sort of person that character is.

> *"Get out of the road, you old fool!" screamed the cruel man to the frail old lady, who was crossing the road slowly.*

It is obvious from his words that the man is impatient and unkind.

✦ The dialogue between the characters shows how they get on with others; how they interact with one another.

✦ You can let the reader know what one character is doing through the words of another character.

> *"Why are you waving that gun around in the air?" the shop assistant asked the robber in a shaking voice.*

In this example, the speech is moving the action forward. It is driving the plot.

✦ When your characters speak, you can provide the reader with subtle clues about their background or where they live. You can choose between different styles of speech for them: between dialect (a way of talking that is particular to a certain area of the country) or standard English and slang or formal.

✦ Withholding the identity of a speaker or speakers from the reader can create suspense.

✦ You can use punctuation marks to indicate the way in which a speaker is talking. To show that a character is shouting, for example, you use an exclamation mark.

> *"Enter!" commanded the king.*

✦ A dash can be used to create a dramatic effect or to emphasise a sudden change of heart. For example:

> *"Your father was a great warrior – and he was also one of my closest friends."*

> *"I'll go to the tree at Hallowe'en – no, on May Day," said Fergus.*

✦ Repeated full stops can show that a speaker is hesitating.

> *'Unless one of you is willing to stand up to the evil beast, I know that tomorrow morning this magnificent hall will be nothing but ... a heap of smouldering ashes."*

> There are helpful hints for children on writing an Irish legend on page 99 of the resource book.

Inuit myths

Myths are stories generated by a culture to explain social customs or to account for natural phenomena. These stories often use supernatural or extremely imaginative terms in their explanations and accounts. Their characters often take part in events in the lives of gods. Myths contain deeper truths relating to life, death, spiritual matters and existence. Unlike legends, myths do not usually contain any historical basis as their source. Traditionally, myths survived and evolved from oral retelling.

To rewrite a myth, it is necessary to have the basic facts in place. Characters' names, the names of places and the basic storyline should not be changed. It is also important that the underlying message is not only retained, but made clear to the reader. If these elements are kept in place, it is possible to create a detailed and imaginative version. Although there is dialogue between characters in myths, it is usually less evident than in other narratives and often takes the form of reported speech.

As myths are generated from a culture's belief system, a lot can be gleaned from these tales about the culture they arise from. From the story of *Sedna* and the scaffolds provided, it can be seen that these myths arose out of their environment and how the Inuit created their culture in response to their environment.

Inuit Culture

The word 'Inuit' means 'the people'. At one time the word 'Eskimo' was used, but this was a Cree Indian word that means 'eaters of raw meat' and is considered a derogatory term. Inuit have an age-old hunting and trapping lifestyle. Although different tribes live in different areas, they share many of the same traditions. The Inuit have a strong oral culture, with stories and myths being passed on since time immemorial. Songs were created for different occasions and could be about anything: hunting experiences, humorous times, starvation, children, poems, mythical beings and predictions of the future. Storytelling is an important element in their culture.

Inuit people are family-orientated. In one household there might be grandparents, aunts, uncles, cousins and adopted children. Everyone is expected to share in all the tasks.

The environment is the driving force of their existence. The Inuit say that the land and snow speak to them. They are subsistence hunters and gatherers and hunt to live and clothe themselves. They believe in sharing what they have with other Inuit. The Inuit would travel vast distances to follow the seasonal movements of the animals and to meet together for special Inuit festivals. This is reflected in the gathering of the tribes for a whale hunt in *Sedna*. A typical view of the great distances experienced by the Inuit can be summed up by a common saying, 'Far away! It's not moving; it will be reached.' This outlook can explain the journey undertaken by the characters in scaffold 1. The long winters, when the Inuit may have spent many weeks inside a small igloo, using the fat from seals to make candles, meant that the coming of light was very important to them. This can be seen in scaffold 2. The Inuit people respect animals and cruelty is not accepted. For example, an Inuit will put a small piece of freshwater ice into a seal hole to let the seals know that they will not be thirsty. This care of animals can also be seen in the *Sedna* story.

Myths

Examples of myths

Myths and Legends retold by Anthony Horowitz (Kingfisher, 1993)
Myths of The Norsemen by Roger Lancelyn Green (Puffin Classics, 1994)
The Illustrated Book of Myths retold by Neil Philip (Dorling Kindersley, 1995)
Myths and Legends of the World by Geraldine McCaughrean (Orion Children's Books, 1995)
Folk Tales and Fables of The Americas and The Pacific by Robert Ingpen and Barbara Hayes (Dragon's World Ltd, 1992)
Heroes, Gods and Emperors by Kerry Usher (Peter Lowe/Eurobook Ltd, 1983)

The children's illustrated version of this myth is on page 106 of the resource book.

Sedna

In the icy wastelands of the Arctic Circle live a race of people called <u>the Inuit</u>[1]. <u>As whales, seals, fish and caribou used to be abundant long ago in the area where they lived,</u>[2] the Inuit would hunt for these creatures in all seasons. Forests grew around the coasts and the Inuit used the wood for fuel and to make tools. The wood was also used to make small one-person boats called kayaks or larger boats called umiaks. These boats were framed with wood and covered with <u>sealskin</u>[3]. The Inuit made their clothes from <u>seal and caribou pelts</u>[3]. <u>If the weather was mild,</u>[4] they lived in tents made out of animal skins. When the <u>dark, harsh</u>[5] winters sent <u>screaming, endless</u>[5] winds <u>rushing</u>[5] across the Arctic plains, the Inuit made earth huts with roofs supported by whale ribs and shoulder blades. When they were on the move hunting, the Inuit made snow houses, called igloos, shaped from blocks of hard snow.

The Inuit lived together in groups that used a common hunting ground, usually near a large bay along the coast. In one of these groups lived a beautiful girl, called Sedna. <u>Sedna had hair as black as sealskin and as shiny as the ice that glinted under the dark night sky.</u>[6] Her hair fell in silky waves to her knees. Sedna's eyes were large and black, but like coals on a fire, they could glow softly or suddenly spark and flash with flames of anger. <u>Sedna was tall and she moved like a shadow of a cloud across the snow, in her soft sealskin dress.</u>[7]

Sedna spent all her time looking after the dogs that pulled the sledges, training them and talking to them. <u>Since Sedna loved the dogs,</u>[8] they followed her wherever she went. With the people in her tribe it was a different matter. With them, Sedna was <u>cold</u>[9] and <u>haughty</u>[9]. All the young men in Sedna's tribal group were in love with her. Whenever her tribe met another, all the young men in that group fell in love with her too. Soon, Sedna's name was whispered with longing throughout the tundra, forests and icepacks of the Inuit hunting grounds. Every day a young Inuit would ask Sedna to marry him. Every day Sedna scornfully refused and returned to her beloved dogs. <u>Rejected, the young men would sit around their smoky fires at night, listening to the howling of the wolves and muttering that Sedna would rather be married to her dogs than to any strong and handsome Inuit male like themselves.</u>[10]

One day, it so happened that many Inuit groups had met together by a large bay to hunt the massive bowhead whales that had been seen there. That night, a group of young men told each other about their love for Sedna. <u>As they spoke,</u>[11] they grew more and more angry about how she had rejected them.

---

1 A myth is anonymous and belongs to a given culture, in this case the Inuit.

2 'As' is a common conjunction. Used at the beginning of this sentence, it signals a subordinate clause that starts the sentence. At the end of this subordinate clause, a comma is used.

3 'Sealskin', 'seal and caribou pelts' and other mentions of how the Inuit use the creatures they hunt, suggests the importance for them of these creatures. This myth tells the tale of how sometimes the hunting is good and sometimes bad. Sedna is a key figure in the success of their hunting.

4 'If the weather was mild,' is a subordinate clause and has a comma to separate it from the main clause.

5 'Dark, harsh', 'screaming, endless' and 'rushing' are all words that could be deleted from this sentence without affecting its meaning.

6 'Sedna had black hair' would be sufficient to convey the meaning of this sentence but the use of similes provides vivid images for the reader.

7 Two sentences have been combined here with the co-ordinating conjunction 'and'.

8 'Since' is a common subordinating conjunction. Used at the beginning of this sentence, it signals that a subordinate clause starts the sentence. At the end of the subordinate clause, a comma is used.

9 'Cold' and 'haughty' convey the same message. They could be substituted by 'proud', 'aloof' or any word that conveys Sedna's feeling of superiority.

10 Three sentences have been combined here by replacing 'they would' with a comma and 'and'.

11 'As they spoke' is a subordinate clause that begins the sentence. It has a comma separating it from the main clause.

"How can she love those dogs more than me?" each one cried. "It isn't normal. She must be <u>bewitched</u>[12] or <u>cursed</u>[12] and it will bring <u>bad luck</u>[12] on all our tribes."

As the night wore on, the young men decided that if they couldn't marry Sedna, then no one was going to. They agreed that they had no choice but to kill her to save their tribes from the misfortune Sedna's strange love for her dogs would bring.

The following day, when the hunters were busy getting ready for the hunt and the dogs had been tied up, the group of young Inuit went looking for Sedna. They found her sitting alone by the stony shore. <u>Before she could ask them what they wanted, they grabbed hold of her and wrapped a strip of sealskin across her mouth.</u>[13] Carrying her as she struggled, they threw her into an umiak, climbed in and pushed out onto the cold, grey sea. A cutting wind threw snow and ice into their stinging faces as they paddled. When they had gone far enough for no one on shore to see them, they lifted Sedna up and threw her overboard. But as she went over the edge, Sedna grabbed hold of the frozen side of the boat and clung on as the umiak rolled and dipped on the heaving waves.

The young men tried as hard as they could to prize Sedna's fingers from the ice-rimmed umiak, but her fingers had stuck fast to the frozen edge. Sedna stared at them in horror as she saw one of the young men pick up an axe. Egged on by the others, the young man chopped off the fingers of Sedna's right hand. Sedna screamed under her sealskin gag, tossing her head right and left in agony. Her long black hair<u>, now soaked with seawater and blood,</u>[14] whipped across the shouting faces leaning over the edge of the umiak. Yelling at Sedna to let go, the young men pulled her hair away from their eyes. As they peered down at Sedna, they saw her fingers floating on the choppy waves. <u>The fingers grew larger and larger and the fingers grew darker and darker.</u>[15] Suddenly, the fingers, one by one, swooped under the surface of the water, turned into seals and darted, twisting and turning away into the ocean.

The young men hit out at Sedna who was still stuck by her left hand to the side of the umiak.

"We knew you were bewitched and bad luck. Get off; get away from us," they howled.

Lifting the axe again, they chopped off the fingers of Sedna's left hand. As the fingers fell into the sea, they turned into walruses, whales and dolphins that leaped and dived and sped away. Sedna, with a last anguished look at the wide white sky above the sea, sank to the ocean floor and <u>became a spirit.</u>[16] In the dim, green, echoing water, Sedna's fingers, now all sea creatures, gathered round her. Her beautiful long black hair streamed like seaweed through the ocean and along the sandy floor. Sedna stood up, swaying with the currents that eddied back and forth. Blood from the stumps where her fingers had been, streaked away in thin wisps until the cold of the water froze the raw flesh. Sedna let out a long low moan that travelled on and on across all the oceans of the world.

<u>Every sea creature heard the sound and came teeming to where Sedna stood.</u>[17] Her dogs on land heard it too. The fur on the back of their necks rose and they stood staring out to sea, baring their teeth and growling ferociously. They saw the young men returning and getting closer to the shore, their faces white with shock. The dogs, smelling Sedna's blood on the axe and with an instinct born out of their love for Sedna, tore onto the

12 'Bewitched', 'cursed' and 'bad luck' all convey the same message. One could be used, deleting the others or all could be substituted.

13 'Before' is a common subordinating conjunction. Used at the beginning of this sentence, it signals that a subordinate clause starts the sentence and so a comma is used after it.

14 'Now soaked with seawater and blood' is a subordinate clause and is separated from the rest of the sentence by commas. This sentence, because it contains a subordinate clause, is a complex sentence.

15 This is a compound sentence because the two main clauses are joined by the coordinating conjunction 'and'. Both parts of the sentence are of equal importance.

16 Myths often express attitudes to life, death, divinity and existence.

17 This sentence has been made into a compound sentence by combining two sentences.

umiak and in a fury ripped the life out of the young men with their teeth. Jumping into the water, the dogs swam to Sedna's side under the sea.

<u>As time went on,</u>[18] Sedna became the Queen of the Underworld and mistress of all living things. She never forgot the cruelty she suffered and her dark eyes flashed with torment and rage at the slightest thing. <u>Every time someone above the sea did something wrong, the sin sank down into the ocean and got caught in Sedna's hair.</u>[19] As she had no fingers, she could not clean it, brush it or dress it. Her once beautiful hair became tangled, filthy and glued with all the evils of the world. <u>Sedna was enraged. She shut away all creatures. No one could fish or hunt.</u>[20]

The Inuit said that the only way to placate Sedna was for someone to travel down to her under the sea. This person had to be a brave, holy person who could talk to spirits. The Inuit call these people shamans. The shaman would have to pass the huge, fierce and faithful dogs that guarded her. The holy person then had to comb out all the sticky sins and bathe Sedna's tangled hair until it was soft and gleaming again. The shaman made two thick plaits for Sedna so that her hair did not float up to the surface and get caught in the fishing nets. As the holy person gently washed and dressed Sedna's hair, she slowly calmed down and relaxed. When the shaman had finished, Sedna was so grateful she freed all the creatures so that humans could hunt, clothe, shelter and feed themselves again.

<u>Sedna is the most important spirit for the Inuit people because she rules whether they live or die.</u>[21]

18 'As time went on' is a subordinate clause at the start of a sentence and so has a comma after it.

19 Myths contain deeper truths and act as an explanation for a culture's beliefs and modes of behaviour. Here it is explained why Sedna reacted so badly and her reaction would act as a warning against wrongdoing on the part of the Inuit.

20 Here the sentences are written in a telegraphic, or shortened, way.

21 Myths have less of a historical basis than legends although they similarly rely on oral retelling and adaptation.

Understanding the grammar and punctuation

Grammar pointers

Combining two or more sentences

Combining two or more sentences involves the addition of clauses to a single clause by using conjunctions.

A simple sentence contains a single clause. For example:

> *Sedna was tall.*

A compound sentence contains two or more clauses joined together with a coordinating conjunction. For example:

> *Sedna was tall **and** she moved like a shadow.*

A complex sentence contains two or more clauses. These clauses consist of a main clause or clauses and a subordinate clause or clauses. For example:

> *When the dark, harsh winters sent screaming, endless winds rushing across the Arctic plains, the Inuit made earth huts with roofs supported by whale ribs and shoulder blades.*

Subordinate clauses develop some aspect of what is being said and are introduced by a subordinating conjunction. Typical subordinating conjunctions include:

> *while, when, although, if, since, before, as, unless, though*

Reordering sentences

To reorder sentences, clauses can be moved around. For example:

> *They lived in tents made out of animal skins if the weather was mild.'*

> *If the weather was mild, they lived in tents made out of animal skins.*

Deleting or substituting words

Many sentences contain more information than is expressed in the main clause. This information can be deleted, leaving a single clause to convey the main meaning. For example:

> *Sedna had hair as black as sealskin and as shiny as the ice that glinted under the dark night sky.*

'Sedna had black hair' would provide sufficient meaning for this sentence, so all other words could be deleted and the words 'hair' and 'black' rearranged to make sense. As the other words could be deleted while retaining meaning, they could also be substituted with different similes.

Writing in more telegraphic ways

Writing in this way often adds an 'abrupt' or urgent feel to the message. It involves dropping any conjunctions and breaking up a complex or compound sentence into simple sentences. For example:

> *Sedna was enraged. She shut away all creatures. No one could fish or hunt.*

Punctuation pointers

Using commas with subordinate clauses

When a complex sentence is rearranged so that the sentence begins with a subordinate clause, a comma is placed after the subordinate clause:

> *If the weather was mild, they lived in tents made out of animal skins.*

The children's version of these notes is on page 109 of the resource book.

Writing feature
Heroes and villains

In traditional stories such as myths, legends and fairytales, the hero or heroine symbolises the triumph of good over evil. The villain is the principal evil character who acts as an antagonist opposed to the hero or heroine.

It is useful for the children to know that these are stereotypical characters and that in many, less traditional, stories the hero/heroine and the villain are more rounded, complex characters. In these stories, characters will not be completely good or evil, although most stories will still create the triumph of good over evil through the development of the story. Sometimes the main character will be an anti-hero who is written as someone who is fairly ordinary and inadequate in certain ways.

The heroes/heroines and villains that appear in traditional stories are 'stock characters', so called because they are easily recognised from recurrent appearances. For example, heroines are beautiful, good and noble. The villains are ugly and wicked and want some form of control or power.

These 'stock characters' are often perceived as archetypes. An archetype recurs in different times and places which suggests that they could therefore embody some essential element of universal human experience.

In the myth 'Sedna', Sedna is portrayed as beautiful and noble in her care for her dogs and her remoteness from the other Inuit. She is therefore written as a stock heroine. However, Sedna has some characteristics that challenge the reader's acceptance of her as a heroine. For example, she is described as 'cold and haughty' with a temper that can make her eyes 'spark and flash with flames of anger'.

By showing that the young men are vain – 'any strong and handsome Inuit male like themselves', we begin to understand why Sedna rejects them. Their conspiracy deepens the reader's response to them as villains until their act of brutality towards Sedna confirms this response. The roles of the hero/heroine and the villain are dependent upon each other. As the young men are Sedna's antagonists and behave in such a terrible way, this places Sedna as the heroine of this myth, arousing our sympathy towards her.

In myths, the archetypes of the hero/heroine and villain demonstrate that these may embody a universal experience of our dealings with other humans. As myths often contain deeper truths about life, the characters of the hero/heroine and the villain often contain deeper truths about human behaviour. To make these deeper truths more accessible to the listener, complexities are often stripped away so that the characters display 'good' or 'evil' in a pure form. Sedna, as a goddess, requires soothing, but she represents the wholly good aspect of nature that supports the Inuit people. The young men behave in a wholly evil way. These villains, typically, get their just deserts.

To help children question their assumptions about hero/heroine and villain characters, try taking 'Goldilocks' to court in the classroom for breaking and entering, wilful damage and theft. Provide Goldilocks with a defence lawyer and the class with a prosecutor. The class can be the jury. During the trial, the children will begin to realise that stereotypical views of heroes/heroines and villains can be challenged.

> There are helpful hints for children on writing an Inuit myth on page 112 of the resource book.

Indian tales

Traditional Indian tales are largely based on folk-tales, myths and legends that are part of the oral tradition. Because most of these stories were created before many people could read or write, they were passed on from generation to generation by word of mouth. Each storyteller would place emphasis on the parts of the story he or she felt were the most important in delivering the message. Consequently, no two storytellers would tell the story in the same way.

Indian tales are usually concerned with the power of faith and the victory of good over evil. Often, reflecting Indian society, the main character will be poor and will have to struggle to survive, overcoming both practical and supernatural difficulties. There are usually both material and moral rewards to be gained, such as wealth, fine clothing, jewellery and a rich lifestyle, happiness and contentment.

There are often references to the climate, landscape, animals and the jobs people do, such as farming, fishing or selling crafts and produce at markets. Because of the intense heat, the threat of drought and famine are common themes occurring in many Indian stories.

Another aspect of Indian storytelling is that of deities, spirits and the supernatural. In addition, the Hindu faith has many gods and goddesses who appear in stories as powerful forces. Usually, a measure of sacrifice on the part of the main character is required in order to pass a 'test' before being rewarded.

Indian tales

Examples of Indian tales

Stories from India by Vayu Naidu (Wayland, 2000)

Folk Tales from India by A K Ramanujan (Random House, 1987)

Hindu Stories – 'Storyteller' series retold by Anita Ganeri (Evans, 2000)

The Bharundu Bird retold by Beula Gandappa (Heinemann, 1995)

Eyes on a Peacock's Tail; Hiss! Don't Bite; The Magic Vessels; A Curly Tale by Vayu Naidu (Tulika Books, 1997)

The Adventures of Young Krishna, the Blue God of India by Diksha Dalal-Clayton (Lutterworth, 1991)

The Elephant-Headed God and other Hindu Tales by Debjani Chatterjee (Lutterworth, 1989)

The children's illustrated version of the story is on page 119 of the resource book.

Sarvar and his stepbrothers

A long time ago in India, there was a young man called Sarvar who lived on a tiny farm where nothing much ever grew.[1] Despite being poor, Sarvar was cheerful, contented, kind and generous. His three stepbrothers, on the other hand, were the opposite. They were nasty, mean and spiteful but, because he was the kind of person who would never think badly of anyone else, Sarvar loved them.[2]

The three stepbrothers didn't like Sarvar at all – his generosity and good spirits made them angry and jealous[3]. One day, Sarvar was told that he had inherited (from his grandfather who had died)[4] a rich, fertile piece of land on which to farm. Sarvar was saddened by his grandfather's death but grateful for his inheritance.

"Come and share my land," he kindly invited his stepbrothers. The stepbrothers rubbed their hands greedily, only too willing to take some of Sarvar's good fortune.

When they saw the land, the stepbrothers took the best pieces for themselves, leaving Sarvar with only a small, dry, rocky patch of ground. Still, Sarvar didn't complain. Instead, he rose each morning, giving thanks for what he had and set out cheerfully to do his work. The three stepbrothers sniggered as they watched Sarvar working hard on the dry land.

"It would take a miracle for anything other than weeds to grow on that!" they jeered.

However, a miracle is exactly what happened. At harvest-time, Sarvar's crop was ten times bigger than that of his stepbrothers. They were astounded by what they saw![5] Sarvar was concerned about their lack of good fortune.

"Take whatever you need from my store," he offered.

Without hesitation, the jealous brothers took everything – all but one sack of grain. Despite their greed, Sarvar did not complain. He gave away the last sack of grain to feed the poor and the sick, living off the last few scraps he could find.[6] Strangely, although he had little left, Sarvar was happier than when his storehouse was bursting with grain.

Soon afterwards, Sarvar and his stepbrothers were called by the District Governor to the city to pay taxes on their land. The mean stepbrothers had no intention of paying their share of the bill. Instead, they formulated a wicked plan to trick Sarvar. They told him that they were taking a trip to the city and asked him if he would like to join them. Sarvar accepted with his usual happy smile and the four men set off.

As soon as they reached the city, the brothers turned to Sarvar and said, "Don't forget to pay your taxes, Sarvar.[7] We only help on **your** land so don't expect **us** to pay!"

1 This is one possible way of opening a story. Alternatively, prepositions such as *in* or *during*, or conjunctions such as *although* could be used for an interesting opening.

2 The comma is used here for two purposes: to separate adjectives describing the stepbrothers and to separate the main clauses from the subordinate.

3 A dash used singly near the end of a sentence to introduce an explanation.

4 The brackets enclose an extra piece of information for the reader.

5 There is often an element of the mystical or supernatural in Indian stories.

6 These simple, descriptive phrases show the contrast between the good and bad elements in the story.

The dash is used here as a pause.

7 The comma has been used here to separate Sarvar's name from the rest of the sentence.

Rather than being angry with his stepbrothers for their unkindness, Sarvar was concerned about embarrassing them because – having given away all of his wealth – he had nothing left to pay the bill.[8] Sarvar fell to his knees in the middle of the square and began to pray that he wouldn't bring shame on his family. Passers-by stopped and stared, curious about this strange man and, by the time the District Governor[9] arrived, a huge crowd had gathered.

The District Governor decided to find out whether Sarvar was as holy as he seemed. Holy men were usually offered food and drink so the District Governor told a guard to take Sarvar a tray upon which he placed a bowl and jug, covered with a cloth. He would soon discover whether Sarvar had miraculous powers as the bowl and jug were empty! The guard handed Sarvar the tray and was astonished when, after Sarvar had blessed the tray and removed the cloth, he saw the bowl was filled with rice and the jug overflowed with milk. Hearing this news, the District Governor sent for Sarvar.

When the three stepbrothers saw Sarvar being taken away, they leapt for joy, shouting, "At last, Sarvar is in trouble!"[10]

How wrong they were. The District Governor gave Sarvar gifts of gold coins, a beautiful robe and a fine horse. The jealous stepbrothers were speechless. They plotted to kill Sarvar and steal his riches. However, the District Governor heard about their plan and had them thrown into jail.

Even after their plot to kill him, Sarvar forgave his stepbrothers and asked that they and the other prisoners be released. The District Governor agreed. The other criminals were so grateful to Sarvar that they vowed to follow his example and live good and honest lives.

Sarvar was saddened by the poverty and sickness he saw in the city. Without a second thought, he gave away his expensive gifts to help the poor and needy. Once again, his stepbrothers saw a way to ruin Sarvar's reputation once and for all. They went straight to the District Governor and told him that Sarvar had deliberately insulted him by giving away his gifts.

How foolish they looked when Sarvar came riding through the streets on the fine horse, wearing the beautiful robe and carrying the sacks of gold coins. Even though Sarvar had never felt comfortable with such riches, he had been rewarded again by God for his kindness and unselfish deeds. From that moment on,[11] Sarvar was always able to help those in need. And his stepbrothers? They had their just rewards by staying poor and unhappy for the rest of their lives.[12]

8 The dashes here are used like parentheses or parenthetic commas, to make the reader stop and think – to remember that Sarvar was now poor again.

9 Note that not all characters are given names. The stepbrothers are essentially anonymous, as are the prisoners. The District Governor is only known by his official title. This sways the reader to having a great affinity with Sarvar, the main character.

10 The prepositional phrase, 'at last' indicates time.

11 This is another prepositional phrase indicating time. A comma is used after the prepositional phrase to separate it from the rest of the information.

12 The ending is both just and moral, a feature of many Indian stories, in which good prevails over bad.

Understanding the grammar and punctuation

Understanding the grammar and punctuation enables children to control the language they use and therefore to write more interesting and powerful stories.

Grammar pointers

Prepositions

Discuss the uses of prepositions in complex sentences. Creative writing can become much more interesting and varied by using prepositions to create different effects. Share the following passage with the children and ask them to suggest alternative prepositions to those underlined. Discuss the effects of the alternative prepositions. Have they altered the sense or meaning of the passage?

> *However, a miracle is exactly what happened. <u>At</u> harvest-time, Sarvar's crop was ten times bigger than that of his stepbrothers. They were astounded <u>by</u> what they saw! Sarvar was concerned <u>about</u> their lack of good fortune.*
>
> *"Take whatever you need from my store," he offered.*
>
> *<u>Without</u> hesitation, the jealous brothers took everything – all <u>but</u> one sack of grain. <u>Despite</u> their greed, Sarvar did not complain. He gave away the last sack of grain to feed the poor and the sick, living off the last few scraps he could find.*

Prepositions can be used to begin stories, taking the reader straight into the action. For example, rather than beginning the story with:

> *A long time ago in India …*

suggest to the children that they might like to choose prepositional phrases such as:

> *In a small village in India …*
>
> *During a drought …*
>
> *Throughout India there was famine …*

Prepositions can also be used to indicate the passage of time (*from that moment on*), possession (*the land had belonged to his grandfather*), position (*in the middle of the square*) as well as direction and accompaniment. Discuss with the children which prepositions would be most appropriate to indicate each of these.

Complex sentences

Remind the children that complex sentences are made up of one or more main clauses and one or more subordinate clauses.

> *Even though Sarvar had never felt comfortable with such riches, he had been rewarded again by God for his kindness and unselfish deeds.*

Explain that the above sentence could be turned into two shorter sentences.

Punctuation pointers

Dashes

Dashes occur singly or in pairs. Used singly near the end of a sentence, they can introduce an explanation or make the final part of the sentence seem dramatic. For example:

> *The three stepbrothers didn't like Sarvar at all – his generosity and good spirits made them angry and jealous.*

A pair of dashes can be used, rather than parentheses or parenthetic commas, to make the reader stop and think before and after a significant piece of information or an aside. For example:

> *Sarvar was concerned about embarrassing them because – having given away all of his wealth – he had nothing left to pay the bill.*

Brackets

Brackets can be used in the same way as parenthetic commas and pairs of dashes to enclose a piece of extra information that is relevant, but of secondary importance, to the main message of a sentence. The information is often factual. For example:

> *One day, Sarvar was told that he had inherited (from his grandfather who had died) a rich, fertile piece of land on which to farm.*

> The children's version of these notes is on page 121 of the resource book.

Writing features
Features of texts from different cultures

Stories from different cultures

Texts from a variety of different cultures provide an insight into the history, society, lifestyles and beliefs of their people. The language used to describe objects, animals, food, clothing and occupations and so on, is a vital element in our understanding of and identification with the characters in the stories.

Discuss with the children the particular words, phrases or descriptions in the exemplar story which make it distinctively Indian in character. Compare these with those words and phrases from stories or poems from other cultures which describe similar objects. Explain to the children that in their own stories, they can bring in references to, for example, the landscape, climate, plants, trees, animals, food and place names that will make their settings more realistic. Authentic voices will also make their characters seem more convincing and powerful so they can include a few dialect terms.

Narrative voice and tense

The opening is important in introducing the characters and creating a sense of time and place. Again, particular words and phrases, authentic names and descriptions of the landscape can be included here to great effect. The third person narrative and past tense are normally used in most traditional Indian tales. Remind the children that it is important to be consistent in their choice of narrative voice and tense to avoid confusing the reader.

Social customs, attitudes and beliefs in Indian tales

In the exemplar story, the main character, Sarvar, is a poor farmer who discovers his own mystical/spiritual powers. This is a common theme, not only in Indian tales, but also in stories from the Caribbean, Africa, China and of the Native American Indians, amongst other cultures. The moral theme of good prevailing over bad is also found in many traditional tales from other cultures. Good characters inevitably receive both material and spiritual rewards while those characters displaying less moral attitudes usually meet a deserving fate.

Many of the issues found in Indian tales can also be found in stories from other cultures and it is important for the children to read a variety of these in order to make connections or comparisons in terms of the ways that social or moral issues are dealt with.

The characters' behaviour, feelings and reactions to events can give insights into the way in which the story may unfold. Ask the children to predict, at strategic points in the story, what might happen next.

There are helpful hints for children on writing an Indian tale on page 124 of the resource book.

Story in letters

Writing a story in letter form allows the writer to use first person narrative from more than one character's point of view. The setting, situation and some information about the characters can be revealed quickly, grabbing the reader's attention and interest from the beginning, with the chain of events unfolding within the context of written communication. The 'hook' needs to come in the first communication, giving clues or hints as to the identities of the characters, their relationship and the potential problem or adventure lying ahead.

The story can be modern, in which case, rather than conventional letter-writing, email could be used as an alternative. Conversely, it could be set in the past, in which case the writer would use the conventions of the chosen era for authenticity.

A variety of story-writing techniques can be used in telling a tale in letter form. For example, humour, irony, angst or a clever twist at the end can keep the reader interested throughout. Particular characteristics such as bravery, faith or jealousy can make the characters believable.

The use of contrast and parallels can help to keep the story moving along. These can take the form of contrasts and parallels between characters, situations, events or settings. Varying the length of the letters, ie some short and some longer, allows the writer to vary the pace of the action taking place.

The plot need not be complex nor too contrived. In fact, ordinary, everyday, realistic situations are more appealing and easier to write about than far-fetched ideas. There should be some challenge or obstacle for the characters to overcome, such as a separation, an argument or the introduction of a third character who causes trouble. The outcome should create a feeling of triumph over the problems, although the ending need not be wholly straightforward.

Stories in letters

Examples of stories in letter form

Dear Greenpeace by Simon James (Walker Books, 1991)

Dear Clare, my ^ex best friend by Ursula Jones (Knight, 1991)

PS Longer Letter Later by Paula Danziger and Ann Martin (Scholastic, 1998)

Snail Mail No More by Paula Danziger and Ann Martin (Scholastic, 1999)

The children's illustrated version of the story is on page 131 of the resource book.

Story in letters

12 Green Crescent
Newtown

27th April 2003

Dear Emily

Roll on the end of these Easter holidays![1] My brother's girlfriend[2] is round here **every day**[3] and I have to be quiet because they're revising for their GCSEs. Why can't they revise at her house? You're really lucky, having no brothers or sisters![4]

[5]I'm really bored without you to go swimming with.[6] I hope you're having fun at your gran's.

Mum says I can have those gorgeous purple sandals I wanted for the summer term. They'll be great if it ever stops raining!

See you soon.

Love
Katie

. . . .

Orchard Cottage
Borchester

30th April 2003

Dear Katie

Thanks for the letter. It's a bit boring at Gran's[7], really. The village is miles from town[8] so I can't even go swimming on my own. Gran keeps nagging me to 'entertain yourself' like she did at my age! I think that means playing with sticks and hoops or skipping ropes. Yuck!

Lucky you, getting new sandals. I have to make do with my old Clarks' ones from last year.[9] Dad is coming down on Friday night and we'll travel home on Sunday. Can't wait to see you at school next week.

Love
Emily

1 Gives a timescale for the setting of the story.

2 Apostrophe of possession.

3 Words written in bold to create emphasis.

4 The reader discovers some of Emily's background through Katie's remarks.

5 A new paragraph is used to introduce a new topic.

6 This gives a hint as to the shared interest of the two friends.

7 Apostrophe of possession. This is short for 'Gran's house'

8 Tells us the location and remoteness of Gran's house.

9 Reveals more of Emily's family situation. 'Clarks' ones' is an apostrophe of possession.

12 Green Crescent
Newtown

6th May 2003

Dear Emily

What's happening? Jake says he was passing your house on his way to his
girlfriend's[10] and there was a 'For Sale' sign in the front garden. You didn't
tell me you were moving![11]

Mrs Harris asked me if you're ill. She needs a note from your dad to say
why you're missing school. I've tried ringing your house but there's no reply
so I'm sending this to your gran's. I wish she had a phone![12]

Please write soon and tell me what's going on.

Love
Katie

● ●

Orchard Cottage
Borchester

10th May 2003

Dear Katie

It's terrible! My dad's firm want him to go and work in Carmouth so we
have to stay at Gran's until the house is sold and Dad can buy one here.
I'm cross with him because he didn't say a word about it until Saturday. He
said he didn't want to upset me. I have to go to school in Carmouth which
means getting up really early because Dad takes me on his way to work
and there's loads of traffic. It's SO embarrassing when his rusty old car
splutters to a halt outside school![13]

I hate being the new girl. I had to stand in front of the class on the first
day and tell them all about myself. They think I have a strange accent and
some of the girls were sniggering. Most of them already go around in
groups and they don't seem to want to make friends.[14] And, if that wasn't
bad enough, I have to sit next to a really[15] swotty BOY[15] called Tom Bowler!
He's shy and hardly says a word and never gets picked for teams in PE.[16] I
wish I was back at Newtown Primary!

Promise you'll write to me.

Love
Emily

10 Apostrophe of possession –
short for 'girlfriend's house'.

11 Irony – neither character was
aware of the events
surrounding their sudden
changed situation.

12 The impact of the story relies
on the geographical distance
between the characters and
letters must be their only
means of communication.

13 Further suggestion to the
reader that Emily's father is
not affluent. The word 'SO' is
in capitals to show emphasis.

14 Introduces the strangeness of
the new situation and the
difficulties encountered in
forming new friendships.

15 In the story, 'Really' is
underlined and 'boy' is in
capitals to create emphasis on
these words.

16 Introduces the idea of a new,
albeit unlikely, friendship
about to be forged.

12 Green Crescent
Newtown

19th May 2003

Dear Emily

School is horrible without you. There was this empty space next to me and, guess what! Mrs Harris has put Jennifer Sowerbutts there. In your place! Mrs Harris said there was no point in Jennifer being on a table by herself when there's room on ours. Oh no! She's so unbearably goody goody and now she's started following me around at playtimes!

Jake's girlfriend has had her belly-button and tongue pierced. I asked my mum if I could have mine done when I'm 16 but she just stared at me as if I was mad. I don't think she approves of Courtney very much[17].

Anyway, Mum says I can have a sleepover in the summer holidays, so please, please come!

Love
Katie

• •

Orchard Cottage
Borchester

26th May 2003

Dear Katie

I asked my dad about coming to your sleepover and he looked a bit unhappy. He muttered something about money not growing on trees because I'm already going on an adventure weekend (that Gran's[18] paying for) with school. Maybe he'll change his mind.

I can't believe Mrs Harris put Jennifer next to you! She never says boo to a goose. Tom is quiet, too. I think he's OK really. We have to do a history project (yawn) in groups and it just so happens that he is brilliant at history! The other two in our group are Samantha and Natasha. They're twins and only ever seem to go around with each other. At least **they** speak to me.

Dad's had an offer on the house so we might be able to move out of Gran's soon. I hope so. I have to share a room with her and she snores!

I miss you.[19]

Love

Emily

17 The teenager's behaviour is seen as exciting and Katie aspires to this trend.

18 This is not an apostrophe of possession; it is a contraction – short for 'Gran is'.

19 This one sentence sums up Emily's loneliness and difficulties in settling into the new school.

12 Green Crescent
Newtown

1st July 2003

Dear Emily

I've seen the 'Sold' sign outside your house! Did you know that
<u>Mrs Harris's husband</u>[20] comes from Carmouth? She told us today.

I can't believe term is nearly over. Do you know yet if you can come to my
sleepover? Jennifer will be coming too, so I hope you don't mind.

Jake's girlfriend, Courtney, has now dyed her hair pink! Mum nearly had a
fit when she saw it.

I was amazed yesterday. We got our reports and mine was 'excellent' for a
change. I came 8th in Maths. Jennifer, as usual, came 1st but Mum was
really pleased with me.

Write back soon.

Love
Katie

• •

Orchard Cottage
Borchester

8th July 2003

Dear Katie

<u>At last!! We're moving to Carmouth</u>[21]. The house is about 5 minutes' walk
from school. That means Dad doesn't have to drive me there any more!
Phew! AND I can go to the leisure centre whenever I want, and pop round
to see Tom and the twins who all live nearby! Dad's firm are going to give
him a pay rise so he might even be able to buy a new car and Gran is
taking me to town after school tomorrow for some sandals as I've finally
grown out of my Clarks' ones.

The really good news is that we'll be coming to Newtown next weekend to
pack everything so Dad says I can definitely come to your sleepover. I can't
wait to see you!

I'm glad you have made friends with Jennifer. Dad seems happier now, so
who knows, I might even be able to invite you both to stay. I'd like you to
meet Tom and the twins. <u>I think you would like them</u>.[22]

See you very soon.

Your friend

Emily

---

20 Use of the apostrophe after a name ending in 's'. It is also correct to write Mrs Harris' husband with just an apostrophe after the 's' in Harris.

21 Short sentences and the use of exclamation marks create a sense of excitement and pace.

22 The story ends on a positive note but is not totally conclusive. The reader may still want to know whether the two characters manage to maintain their friendship.

Understanding the grammar and punctuation

Understanding the grammar and punctuation enables children to control the language they use and therefore to write more interesting and powerful stories.

Grammar pointers

Paragraphs

In letter-writing, we use paragraphs to make it easy for the reader to follow the development of an idea or a line of argument. Paragraphs that are too long make the story difficult or boring for the reader. On the other hand, rapid sequences of very short paragraphs can have a staccato or choppy effect – but this is good when the writer wants to create a sense of excitement.

Beginning a new paragraph

As a general rule, begin a new paragraph each time a new idea, piece of information or the next event in the plot is introduced.

Linking paragraphs

Particularly in informal letters, connectives can be used to link ideas or highlight contrasts. For example, 'besides' or 'after all' can serve to emphasise an idea or train of thought.

Punctuation pointers

The apostrophe for possession

Remind the children about the rules for using the apostrophe.

When there is one owner, place an apostrophe followed by the letter 's' after the owner. For example:

the girlfriend of Jake

becomes

Jake's girlfriend

When there is more than one owner, plural owners, place the apostrophe after the 's'. For example:

the father of the twins

becomes

the twins' father

Some plural words do not end in 's'. To show possession with these words, use an apostrophe followed by an 's'. For example:

the books of the children

becomes

the children's books

The apostrophe with proper nouns ending in 's'

You can show possession in the normal way, by adding an apostrophe and then an 's'. For example:

the sister of Mrs Harris

becomes

Mrs Harris's sister

Or you can choose to follow the name with an apostrophe but leave out the additional 's'. For example:

Mrs Harris' sister

Showing possession with 'it'

You do not use an apostrophe to show possession with the word 'it'. You merely use an 's'. For example:

the eyes of it were red

becomes

its eyes were red

> The children's version of these notes is on page 135 of the resource book.

Writing features
Narrative viewpoint in letter stories

Explain to the children that if we tell a story in the first person, the reader shares the thoughts and feelings of the narrator and generally feels close to the character. In a story where two characters write in the first person, we are able to see events from both points of view and share two sets of feelings, anxieties, innermost secrets and so on. The use of two first person narrators also enables the story to unfold through their adventures/situations.

Go over the differences between informal and formal letter-writing and how style and tone affect the way we speak and write in both informal and formal situations. Look at examples of both types of letter to highlight those differences; for example letters from solicitors and letters to and from friends or relatives.

Once the children have grasped the concept of formal versus informal letter-writing, discuss the possibility of setting their stories in the past, present or future and the implications of authentic language style in addition to the use of technology, such as email, as a means of communication.

Explain to the children how their writing can become more interesting by highlighting contrasts and parallels between characters and situations.

In the sample story, the two characters, Katie and Emily, are from similar, single parent families. Katie has a teenage brother, whereas Emily is an only child. Emily's father is experiencing problems of moving to another area, along with some economic difficulties, whereas Katie's mother is coping with the problems of teenagers.

The friendship of the characters is revealed through their mutual loneliness when Emily moves away. The difficulties of both characters in forming new friendships are parallel, as are the unlikely friendships they eventually begin to forge, while retaining their own strong bond.

The setting also has contrasts – Newtown is provincial and modern with amenities close to hand, whereas Borchester is a quiet, remote village, some distance from the nearest town.

The characters' feelings are important to the story and again, contrasts and parallels can add interest, conflict, tension and atmosphere.

The time span of the story can also play an important part in revealing the characters' feelings and, in particular, how those initial feelings may begin to change. In the sample story, Katie and Emily's letters express their anxieties and responses are close together. Gradually, as the two characters come to accept the changed situation, the letters become spaced further apart.

There are helpful hints for children on writing a story in letters on page 138 of the resource book.